THE SCOTTISH LIBRARY

THE SCOTTISH LIBRARY

CONTEMPORARY SCOTTISH VERSE
Edited by Norman MacCaig and Alexander Scott

SCOTTISH SHORT STORIES 1800-1900
Edited by Douglas Gifford

JAMIE THE SAXT
A Historical Comedy by Robert McLellan
Edited by Ian Campbell and Ronald D.S. Jack

SCOTTISH PROSE 1550-1700
Edited by Ronald D.S. Jack

THE SCOTTISH LIBRARY

General Editor: Alexander Scott

THE BURNING

A Play by

Stewart Conn

CALDER & BOYARS

LONDON

First published in Great Britain in 1973
by Calder & Boyars Ltd
18 Brewer Street London W1

© Stewart Conn 1973

ISBN 0 7145 0831 4 Cloth Edition

This volume has been produced with the assistance of the
Scottish Arts Council and the publishers wish to acknowledge
with thanks the substantial help given not only by the Council
itself but by its Literature Committee without which this
volume and others in the series could not be viably published.

Printed in Great Britain by
Biddles Ltd
Guildford, Surrey

To Bill Bryden

For it is written in the Scriptures, that God sendes Legions of Angells to guarde and watch over his elect.

(James VI: <u>Daemonologie</u>)

On this earth there are pestilences and there are victims, and it's up to us, so far as possible, not to join forces with the pestilences.

(Albert Camus: <u>The Plague</u>)

Toutes les choses terribles au monde commencent avec des petites lâchetés.

(Dr. Adelaide Hautval)

AUTHOR'S NOTE

The Burning did not spring from any predisposition on my part towards Scots historical drama; but from what struck me as the theatrical potential of the theme, and its relevance today. Our own age is as 'mocking and hostile' as that of James and Bothwell; as brutal towards those caught in the middle of any battle of creeds, or for power; and as ready to identify 'evil' with the other side.

Much of the play's incident is drawn from historical sources, among them James's own Daemonologie. Liberties have naturally been taken with the attitudes of the characters - and with chronology. It proved necessary, during the lengthy process of revising the play, to take a committed line on the 'witches'. If any apology is due, it is to the ghost of Bothwell.

(Bothwell incidentally is not the husband of Mary Stuart, but their nephew Francis Stewart-Hepburn, fifth earl and cousin to King James.)

There is no attempt at a reconstruction of 16th century speech. I have aimed at the idea rather than the reality; at a hardness of diction, yet suppleness of rhythm, capable of suggesting the period and coping with the play's contemporary concepts - while remaining clearly intelligible. In speaking the lines, the use of the letter t should be closely observed (as in the substitution of -it for -ed in the past participle, eg: wantit for wanted, intendit for intended). If the language can be thought of as a leather belt, this sound provides the studs that hold it in place.

In visual terms too, any presentation of the play must resist sentimentality or over-elaborateness. Costumes should be functional, not merely decorative. I envisage the stage being as bare as possible - where practicable, completely bare.

THE BURNING

This play was first presented by the Royal Lyceum Theatre Company of Edinburgh, on 18th November 1971, with the following cast:

PRIEST	Martin Cochrane
HERALD TO THE KING	Brown Derby
DAVID SEATON, DEPUTE BAILIFF	Joseph Brady
THE MINISTER OF TRANENT	Bryden Murdoch
JAMES VI OF SCOTLAND	Derek Anders
LORD MAITLAND, HIS CHANCELLOR	Paul Kermack
LORD HOME	Michael Harrigan
FRANCIS HEPBURN, EARL OF BOTHWELL	John Cairney
THE KING'S JESTER	John Grieve
SIM	Martin Cochrane
CRAW	James Kennedy
DR FIAN	John Shedden
EFFIE MCCALYAN	Ros Drinkwater
GILLES DUNCAN	Jeni Giffen
THOMAS STRACHAN, SMITH	Bill McCabe
OFFICER TO THE KING	Ian Ireland
JUDGE	Ian Stewart
DEMPSTER	Hugh Evans
SCRIVENER	Andrew Abrahams
WOMEN	Renée Blair
	Sandra Clark
	Claris Erickson
	Maureen Jack

The play was directed by Bill Bryden

The action takes place in the Kingdom of Scotland, towards the end of the 16th century

ACT ONE

Prologue

(A raised altar, upstage.
Huge candles, a cross. Two cloaked figures enter,
each bearing a chalice. The chalices placed cere-
monially on the altar. Other figures enter, among
them a hooded PRIEST: he takes position at the altar,
while the others kneel as though praying silently. All
formal, like a dream)

PRIEST. (intones)

        sake Jesu's   swete for
        gane be will ever   Joye the me grant
        Damnatioun   endless and
        Shame wardly and   Sinne frae me keep
        Passioun bitter Thy   for Lord thou
        slae felon the   frae me keep
        Kingdome His to   dead and quick baith
        doom to there and   come us bade He
        Ghost Holy the   of gotten was
        Christe Jesu Sonne   dear His to and
        nochte of all and   Eard and Heavin baith
        wrochte that God Almychty   in trow I

(During the responses, the figures drink in turn)

(Loudly)

Believe not in God

VOICES. We believe not in God

PRIEST. Nor in Christ His Son

VOICES. Nor in Christ His Son

PRIEST. But in HIM

VOICES. But in HIM

PRIEST. Ever do his bidding

VOICES. Ever do his bidding

PRIEST. Breaking not bread

VOICES. We break not bread

PRIEST. But rendering up the flesh

VOICES. Render up the flesh

PRIEST. In honour of HIM

ALL. In honour of HIM

(The PRIEST'S arms raised, as in benediction.
Tableau: a mediaeval wood-cut)

PRIEST. all you with be Christ
Jesus Lord our of grace the

(The chalices are drained)

VOICES. our of grace...
our of grace...
our of grace...

(The figures fan out as a WOMAN is brought forward.
She carries a CHILD. The CHILD is prepared for
baptism. The PRIEST withdraws the cross: it is a
ceremonial sword, its pommels studded. The figures
weave. The WOMAN is held. The sword is raised.

The chant reaches its climax. The sword plunges.
The WOMAN shrieks. BLACKOUT)

(A spot comes up on the HERALD)

HERALD. (reads from a scroll): PROCLAMATION -

The Royal Majestie and Three Estates in Parliament
being informit of the dire and abominable superstitioun
of Witchcraft, Sorcery and Necromancy in times
bygone against the law of God,

and for the avoidance and away-putting of all such
vain superstitioun in time to come,

it is hereby statute and ordainit by the Royal Majestie
and Three Estates aforesaid that no manner of person
of whatsoever degree is to take upon hand in any times
hereafter any manner of Witchcraft, Sorcery or
Necromancy, nor give themselves furth to have any
such craft nor knowledge thereof,

nor that no person seek help, response nor any
consultatioun at the hands of such aforesaid users,
under pain of death:-

and this to be put into execution by the Justice Sheriffs,
Stewards, Bailiffs, Lords of Regality and Royalty,
their Deputes, and other Judges competent within this
Realm with all rigour having power to execute the same.

And this by Act of Parliament.

Scene 1

(Near Tranent. A log bridge over a swollen stream.
A thunderstorm. Looking into the water, a man in
hodden grey, with a bonnet: DAVID SEATON, depute-
bailiff. A huddled figure enters: the MINISTER. Each
has a lantern)

13

MINISTER. Have you lost your senses? (As SEATON turns)
    To stay out in this?

SEATON. We have dug ditches, lest the stream rise and
    destroy the crops, as last year. (Looks down again)
    It is less in spate now. God be thankit. (Pause)
    Yourself, Minister?

MINISTER. Putting up prayers for the miller's son, that
    is sick.

SEATON. Not the pestilence?

MINISTER. The great sweirness, more like! Causit by
    lying in bed past noon. Instead of giving assistance
    to his father.

SEATON. He will recover?

MINISTER. He is in God's hands. Already the Papists have
    attemptit to treat him, with their herbs and simples.
    (Smugly) That were soon put a stop to.

    (Roll of thunder, not too near. The Minister glances
    up)

    The storm is almost past. (Pause) What is it,
    Master? What are you seeking?

SEATON. My... maidservant... Gilles Duncan...

MINISTER. She is never out in this?

SEATON. I fear she may be.

MINISTER. For what purpose?

SEATON. These past three weeks, she has absentit herself
    from under my roof, alternate nights. Most like, she
    trysts with some lad.

MINISTER. That were illicit. (Pause) There are tales
    abroad in Tranent, of this Gilles Duncan's potency to

14

heal the sick. By the laying-on of hands.

SEATON. Creditable, if scarce credible.

MINISTER. Where there is potency to heal, there is also
potency to hurt. By unnatural means. If she is again
absent, the Session must be alertit.

SEATON. It concerns the Session!

MINISTER. More than the Session.

(Thunder)

Does that mean nothing? Do you not know, to what
King James credits these storms?

SEATON. The King!

MINISTER. He says they are causit by witches in his kingdom. (As SEATON laughs) Hear me out! When
James set sail for Denmark, to collect his royal bride,
tempests tore the canvas from his vessels, split their
masts and drove them from their moorings. Crushing
the hulks like tinder. Another, loadit with princely
jewels, was sent to the bottom, off Leith. The ancient
Greeks blamit Neptune. James accuses Satan.

SEATON. Behind the storm, witchcraft?

MINISTER. And behind that, the Black Earl.

SEATON. Bothwell!

MINISTER. So, there is significance outwith ourselves.

SEATON. She is but a lass. She would never have truck
with such —

MINISTER. You are depute-bailiff. (As SEATON nods)
And would rise to bailiff? (Pause) See you make your
report.

SEATON. If she is innocent?

MINISTER. The Lord will look after His own.

SEATON. This is on my conscience.

MINISTER. There is also your duty. Take care the demands
of the one do not blind you to the dictates of the other.
Else I should not care to answer for you.

SEATON. Sir, I am prepared to answer for myself.

MINISTER. Before God?

SEATON. Before God.

MINISTER. And the King?

SEATON. And the King.

(The MINISTER exits. SEATON looks round, pulls
his plaid about him)

Scene 2

(Holyrood. A chair of state. Banners, drapeaux.
The KING stands on the throne, a sword in his hand.
Before him, an ATTENDANT. SIM and CRAW look
on. The ATTENDANT kneels. The KING scratches
vigorously at his codpiece. He raises the sword,
lowers it)

KING. Thou art hereby, heretofore and hereinafter ordainit,
dubbit and proclaimit: Freeman of the Grassmarket,
Warden of the Lawnmarket, Grandmaster of the Fish-
market, the Fleshmarket and the Saltmarket, Great
Stinker of the Fartmarket, Farter of the Stinkmarket,
Defender of the King's Faith, the King's Breastplate
and the King's Codpiece (He scratches) and all that lie
therein...

(He dubs the ATTENDANT)

Arise Sir Silly Smiddy, Seigneur of Tosspots,
Champion of Pishpots... It is now our kingly wish
that thou shouldst kiss... our ring!

(The KING turns his back. A raspberry, as the
ATTENDANT kicks him. SIM and CRAW jig round
the throne)

SIM. Matthew, Mark, Luke and John
Bless the wench the King lies on...

CRAW. Genesis, Exodus, Leviticus, Numbers,
Watch over King James's nightly slumbers...

(The KING joins them)

KING. Amo, amas, amat...
Amamus, amatis... Ah cant!

(He clutches himself. Laughter. The ATTENDANT
gestures, exits. The KING crosses to the throne,
spits on it and pretends to polish it. Sounds, off. He
drops his sword, has to pick it up, trips. He giggles.
He is in fact KING JAMES'S JESTER. JAMES himself
enters: wearing a doublet with a white ruff. Well
padded. Unshapely legs. With him: LORD MAITLAND
his Chancellor, LORD HOME, the HERALD, The
OFFICER as bodyguard)

MAITLAND. No castle can hold him long.

HOME. Dispose of him.

HERALD. There is no proof against him.

HOME. His reputation is enough.

HERALD. He paints himself larger than life, among the
gullible.

HOME. He has made attempts on the King's person.

17

JAMES. And that of our affectionate bedfellow the Queen...
    (He toys with the feathers of his codpiece: the
    JESTER, who has with the others cleared the central
    playing area, mimics him and stifles a laugh, then
    turns away as JAMES continues) You cannot have a
    man put down, without proof having been found against
    him.

HOME. Enough is known, to incriminate him.

MAITLAND. Not just incriminate, but utterly destroy.

JAMES. Justice must be seen to be done. Else his minions
    will await his return. Calling his spirit corporeal.
    He must be treatit with the full force of the Law; his
    guilt held up to the light. Which he blots out, like a
    black spider.

HOME. But you plan to set him free!

MAITLAND. So that we can ensnare him.

HERALD. If he is the threat you say.

HOME. You defend him?

HERALD. Scarce my function. (To JAMES) I bring news
    from Tranent. Anent a servant maid Gilles Duncan—

HOME. This is no time -

    (But JAMES raises a hand, for the HERALD to continue)

HERALD. She has been reportit to the session, after
    injunction from the pulpit. In consequence of village
    squabbles, guaranteeing one party injury against
    another.

MAITLAND. Be specific.

HERALD. There is reportit potency in healing the sick.
    Plus matters bordering on the miraculous.

18

MAITLAND. She has been interrogatit?

HERALD. Not yet.

JAMES. Tranent is near North Berwick. Where were cast those spells against our person. (To HOME) Here is the chink in Bothwell's armour, through which he will be deliverit up. Release him now, he will take advantage of the next full moon. To manipulate our overthrow. But we shall have him. (He circles the stage) Bothwell is a bloody hell-bent creature, that has no care for those he drags to purgatory with him. A dark rider, on a dark mount. It befits him to perish in a desert of flaming sand - as all that are violent against God. There shall he lie, defiant in death as in life, like Capaneus obdurate under judgment. (Sits on the throne) It only grieves us to think how many must perish, through him.

HERALD. Must they?

JAMES. It is in accord with Scripture. We are the Lord's anointed, and sacred the breadth of the Realm. Is there not about us a ring of stalwart servants, in whom we trust? And have done, since the unkindly murder of our mother the Queen?

HERALD. You are hard on Hepburn.

MAITLAND. Hepburn is what he is.

HERALD. He has the blood royal.

   (JAMES contorts)

MAITLAND. But no fit claim to the throne.

HERALD. My suspicion is, he would be satisfied as second in the land.

MAITLAND. He has no right!

HOME. His time draws near.

HERALD. (turns on HOME) I smell pettiness. Against a better swordsman than yourself.

HOME. How dare you!

HERALD. The last time you and Bothwell met in the High Street, did he not— ?

HOME. (enraged) We were outnumbert three to one.

HERALD. Not the story I heard.

(HOME takes a furious step towards the HERALD. The HERALD pushes him back. HOME'S hand flies to his swordhaft. The JESTER jinks betwen them, with his own sword)

JESTER. Now, now, Lordships...never nakit steel...in the King's presence...(To HOME) You'll have to learn to keep your tempers, or it'll get you into trouble.

(HOME pinions him)

MAITLAND. The King could have you hangit.

JESTER. (to JAMES) Never fash, Majesty...it's only made of wood...like Home's head...(As HOME twists his arm) ouch...Majesty...

JAMES. Release him...my Lord.

JESTER. You heard what the mannie said...

(Reluctantly, HOME obeys)

HOME. (to the HERALD) The next time, you will pay...

JAMES. What...if Bothwell should suspect our motive?

MAITLAND. A sum will be demandit for his release.

JAMES. Substantial.

MAITLAND. He knows the state of the coffers.

JAMES. He is responsible!

MAITLAND. (a slight glance at HOME) As are we all.

JAMES. Let conditions be drawn up.

MAITLAND. That has been done.

JAMES. All that remains is for Bothwell...to be brought...
     (He rubs his hands together) and humblit...

MAITLAND. Bothwell is here.

     (HOME's hand steals to his sword. MAITLAND
     smiles)

JAMES. He was secure...

MAITLAND. He is secure...

JAMES. ...in Tantallon.

MAITLAND ...no longer in Tantallon.

JAMES. Here? (MAITLAND nods) In...Holyrood?
     (MAITLAND bows) Well then... (JAMES has to
     clear his throat) Let us...have him in! (As the
     ATTENDANTS turn) Wait! (Then with a show of
     casualness) let us first...read the conditions...
     (And the parchment is handed to him:) Aaaah...
     aaaaaah...yes, excellent...He...aaaaah...is bound?

MAITLAND. Sire.

HOME. And has a gauntlet to run.

JAMES. (loudly) Bring him in!

     (JAMES hands back the parchment, adjusts his dress,
     adopts a regal posture. Tableau. BOTHWELL is
     brought in, roped. He bows. SIM and CRAW watch

the scene, but without impinging on it. BOTHWELL
breaks the silence)

BOTHWELL. I bow to one fool, the other bows back: on
one hand, the King's Fool; on the other, the Fools'
King!

MAITLAND. To think the Bishop of Durham spoke of this
noble's 'social graces and attainments'.

BOTHWELL. I have a complaint——

MAITLAND. Later!

BOTHWELL. (ignores him) —— about the porridge, in
Tantallon Castle.

MAITLAND. There is a paper, his Grace would first have
you sign.

BOTHWELL. Putting on weight again, cousin... or are you
just well paddit?

JAMES. It is our wish——

BOTHWELL. Or your Chancellor's.

JAMES. ——that you be releasit——

BOTHWELL. What surety?

JAMES. ——on surety of good behaviour——

BOTHWELL. The terms?

MAITLAND. A sum will be ——

BOTHWELL. You must be short of silver.

MAITLAND. I recall your promise to feed this Court at the
rate of two hundred thousand crowns per annum,
without expense to his Grace of one farthing.

BOTHWELL. By bleeding Elizabeth, not turning out my own pocket.

MAITLAND. Elizabeth will relish that, when next you play lapdog to her.

BOTHWELL. If I reject your offer?

MAITLAND. Your estates are forfeit.

BOTHWELL. How is my silver to be usit?

JAMES. Towards furtherance of peace throughout the Realm. Our intent is to put down all warring factions, and dominate the northern nobles utterly. To banish from our house all Jesuits and Papists, and command full obedience to our Acts of Parliament. Through Maitland here at our right hand, we treat with Elizabeth, that our enemies be deliverit into our hands. On behalf of that course we shall share common foes unto death - in despite of the Pope, and the King of Spain, and all Leaguers - and the Devil their Master.

(Pause)

BOTHWELL. (quietly) A costly house to put in order.

JAMES. Our position is God-given, and a divine duty.

MAITLAND. While you are but England's errand-boy.

BOTHWELL. An errand-boy who holds the key to the Border.

MAITLAND. Errand-boys should learn to serve the one master.

BOTHWELL. I do, Chancellor...I do...

(Pause)

JAMES. It is right you should serve us, who rule this land by policy.

23

BOTHWELL. Policy demands wisdom.

JAMES. There are our councillors. Besides, the King is the true child and servant of God. Wisdom is investit in him, through heavenly grace. He has the key to the nation's safety.

BOTHWELL. A King should not shiver at the sight of steel.

HOME. It is discourteous to cite that. It was instillit in the King in the womb, when those men burst into his mother's chamber to despatch David Rizzio.

BOTHWELL. His legs got bent, at the same time!

MAITLAND. King James has a position in this Realm. He approaches the prime of his years and vigour; is alliet with a potent prince, heir to a mighty kingdom, dominant in Europe. It is not meet he be beardit in his Court by any jackanapes baron that feels himself outdone.

BOTHWELL. A pity so great a sovereign should have as Chancellor an empty puddock-stool of a knight.

MAITLAND. You forget one thing. You are in the King's power.

BOTHWELL. What power? (He beckons the JESTER forward) He has but the appearance of power. Its illusion. Not power itself. Or its basis. (He takes the JESTER's wooden sword) Here is your illusion, cousin. It has the trappings. But lacks the ring of metal. Instead, it is soft and pliable... Able to be manipulatit, but without a cutting edge. It remains a plaything... a Fool's bauble, a wee boy's toy... or an appurtenance for ladies. Never for a grown man, far less a sovereign at the height of his vigour. You wield this Chancellor, as he wields you. You make gestures of kingship. Nothing more. You are all pageant and procession. Your monarchy is a monkey-like masquerade. The whole base of your power, a pretence, to be snappit at will.

(He is about to break the sword across his knee)

JESTER. Hey!

(But it is JAMES who intervenes, takes it)

JAMES. The weapon may be weak. In hands that wear
fetters. In ours, it is investit with puissance
beyond itself. The Right is on our side. In any
battle we engage. You call this blade puny, and
deride it? Behind it lie our birthright and the
traditions of the Court. Through God's heavenly
guidance, we command obeisance. This is a mighty
weapon, manifest through God, and Christ our
Saviour.

(He flourishes the sword. The JESTER takes it from
him)

JESTER. Here... You'll do yourself an injury...

JAMES. There are other ways to govern, than by violence.
We shall rule Scotland by a Clerk of the Council,
which others have not been able to do with the sword.

BOTHWELL. Wait till you draw your dagger across Moray's
cheek. Or head for Hampton Court, leaving behind
the stench of rotting flesh.

JAMES. You offend all decency.

BOTHWELL. It is you! With your feminine fancies and
lewd lures. (As JAMES grows more and more upset)
With your scribbling... and your... snivelling...

(JAMES responds as though struck. The JESTER
supports him)

JAMES. You are an evil man. And you will be put down.
Who are neither true Protestant nor Catholic... and
have nothing... but secret and unholy ambition.

BOTHWELL. I have the one thing you lack, cousin...
popularity.

MAITLAND. Easy bought.

BOTHWELL. Less easy kept. For all the fripperies you
dole out. The sweetmeats and strips of land. (To
JAMES) Where you curry favour, I command it.
Through the lealty of my people. That is my strength.

MAITLAND. It will soon change. (To the HERALD) Let
him hear the conditions.

HERALD. (reads) 'On leaving this place, you are to remain
in house or estate, notifying the King's Lieutenant of
any journey of three miles or more abroad. Second,
you will avoid public meeting-places, and all con-
gregation of above one dozen persons. Third, you will
employ as household staff not above sixteen of either
sex, and these not accoutred bondsmen, but common
hirelings... (With added stress: meanwhile MAITLAND
smiling) ...without debt to your blood or lineage.
Nor is any residence to be fortified; but remain open
to inspection by the King's Lieutenant at whatsoever
hour he pleases. Finally you may not linger in any
public place between sunset and sunrise. Under pain
of dispossession. This last being the most crucial of
the terms laid down.'

(The parchment is returned to MAITLAND)

BOTHWELL. That all? Last time, I was to 'prove another
man in time coming.'

JAMES. Better improve the one you already are.

MAITLAND. His Grace's terms are, as has been——

BOTHWELL. The style is stiltit. It could only be yours.
Or that blind pedant your father's.

MAITLAND. You sound keen to return to Tantallon.

BOTHWELL. That would not do. The King must have me
releasit. In Tantallon, he'd find me too hot to handle.
It would demand too many soldiery. That are needit

elsewhere. The freedom the King offers me, is
forcit on him.

MAITLAND. You despise freedom so?

BOTHWELL. What is the exchange? From a sandstone
cell six paces square, to a cage the size of Scotland,
with as many bars as there are King's men! (Pause)
Still, I have a freedom of sorts. Freedom of thought,
and sentiment. Freedom of affection. Which is a
man's real freedom. That is something you could
never understand, who want your subjects to conform,
to support your State and attend your Kirk. To be
dominatit, utterly. (Pause) If you could, you'd
control their dreams.

MAITLAND. Yours are your own, thank God.

BOTHWELL. (to JAMES) Yours, cousin? No dark shadows
there?

MAITLAND. Greater shadows than Bothwell. The Pope.
And Philip. You have forgot to sign.

BOTHWELL. My word is not acceptit, as bond?

JAMES. (a puny figure, in the throne) No.

(MAITLAND smiles, shakes his head. BOTHWELL
sighs. He signs with a flourish)

BOTHWELL. What will you be doing, cousin, while I am...?

JAMES. We shall repair three days hence to our fortress
of Fife. From Leith, by royal barge. Complete with
entourage.

JESTER. To gralloch the red deer. That cannot defend
themselves.

MAITLAND. (sees the signature) Take him away!

BOTHWELL. If all the fools in the world were wise men,
and the wise men fools...

JESTER. It would make little difference.

BOTHWELL. At least there is one, knows his station.

JAMES. Before you go...do you frequent...the east sector of the Kingdom?

BOTHWELL. Seldom. There is a snell wind there, they tell me...

JAMES. Yes, snell...

BOTHWELL. We will meet again, cousin... never fear...

(BOTHWELL is taken out. HOME turns to JAMES, whispers urgently)

HOME. Was it wise to say we would sail from——?

JAMES. We said in three days time. By design. We shall defeat his purpose, by setting out furthwith.

HOME. I dislike his being releasit.

HERALD. You heard the conditions!

JAMES. As he says, it is the freedom of the walled garden. He is a stag, and will soon be at bay. Like Actaeon, destroyit by his own hounds.

JESTER. (returns from having seen BOTHWELL depart) Can we come with you to Fife, Majesty?

MAITLAND. Beware lest we set a pair of antlers on your brow and whip you through the wood for sport.

JESTER. Save your rhetoric. Enough's been spilt for the one day.

JAMES. Put foot on the soil of our Court within thirty days, you will indeed be whippit.

(JAMES exits)

28

HERALD. (holds out the parchment) What of this?

> (MAITLAND takes the parchment, tears it across, lets the pieces flutter to the floor. All exit, except the JESTER. He steps forward, and is joined by SIM and CRAW. SIM makes a ball of the torn parchment, bowls it at the JESTER who uses his sword as a bat. CRAW fields)

SIM. A fine instrument, you have there.

CRAW. What you could cry...a comely blade!

JESTER. Or a tough tool... (Holding it in front of him) that has done sturdy work in its day.

SIM. Sturdy or turdy?

CRAW. Careful, you'll give her a skelf!

SIM. I hope you find a clean scabbard for it.

CRAW. Look who's talking.

SIM. Craw doesn't mind where he planks his. Do you, Craw?

CRAW. As bad as that Bothwell...they say he doesn't even stop to dry it in atween

JESTER. In atween what?

> (Laughter)

SIM. Mind you...a man has to stop some time...or he'll do hissel an injury...

JESTER. Don't you believe it. Craw's been at it steady for the past ten years.

SIM. Aye, and look at him!

CRAW. You're just jealous.

SIM. Could give you six inches of a start. Seriously, though. I mean...they say Both-well has a...superhuman capacity.

JESTER. That's why his Kingship gets so upset. He doesnae have a look in.

CRAW. Doubt if he ever gets anything else in, either. They say... (Looks round) he's got...a carbuncle on it. That's why he keeps... (Scratching gesture)

SIM. His isnae big enough to haud a carbuncle!

JESTER. One day he'll waken up and find it's disappeart.

SIM. Fell aff, more like!

JESTER. I'm telling you ——

SIM. Who's asking?

JESTER. ——there's more to that Bothwell, than meets the eye.

CRAW. Exactly.

JESTER. He doesnae scare easy, for a start.

CRAW. More than you can say for his Prissiness.

SIM. Say that again.

CRAW. More than you can say for——

SIM. (to JESTER) Hie...you're not thinking of...

JESTER. Thinking of what?

SIM. ...well, taking up with Bothwell, are you?

JESTER. No me. I ken whit side my bread's buttert!

(They sing)

30

SONG. THE BAULD WINDS BLEW

The bauld winds blew, the fire-flauchts flew,
   The sea ran tae the sky,
For the thunder growled, the sea-dogs yowled,
   As they gaed scourin by.

For storms blew up, and rains cam doon,
   On King James and all his men;
But whether sent by witches or no,
   They honestly didna ken.

The King's bark crossed the pearly Forth,
   Wi whitna pearly prow;
When it couldna speil the brow o the waves
   It needled them through ablow.

O the King frae regal seat was tossed
   And piteously did roar;
For a vulgar part o his bodie
   Cam thud upon the floor.

Yet soon the Fifeshire coast was won
   And he mounted his steed o wind;
And he headed him to fair Falkland
   And left the shore ahint.

So in the fertile land o Fife,
   They rade to catch the deer...

(last couplet spoken)

While in the village o Tranent
   David Seaton had things to speir.

Scene 3

(Outdoors, Tranent. THE MINISTER, SEATON.
Birdsong. The MINISTER carries a Bible)

MINISTER. You have actit wisely, Master.

SEATON. In whose eyes?

MINISTER. All. Including your own.

SEATON. If we are in error?

MINISTER. That will be revealit, at the questioning. Evil
must be brought to book.

SEATON. You make her out to be already guilty.

MINISTER. So she is. Till and unless her innocence shine
like a light.

SEATON. She is of honest parentage.

MINISTER. There is an evil in this land, that propagates
in every shire, never showing its face but undermining
the structure of the state, like a warren.

SEATON. She...attends the Kirk.

MINISTER. Did not Antide Colas confess she did attend
midnight prayer on Christmas eve, then go to a profane
meeting, only to return to break holy bread at dawn?
No wonder the Inquisitors have been sore exercisit in
dealing with such gross offence, when it matures
within the marrow of the body politic, the very kernel
of the Kirk.

SEATON. We deal with a simple country lass.

MINISTER. We deal with a Beast. Foreign to the laws of
God's kingdom. And the decencies of His people.
God is so vigilant for the weale of His own, that he
disappoints the will of those that conspire against His

holy throne. By this same power have been put down of late, here in Lothian, a number of ungodly creatures little better than devils. That have arisen in guise of innocence, like this 'simple lass'. They have entert into league with the Devil, in their souls' despite.

SEATON. It is surely never God's will that——

MINISTER. It is not for you to question God's will. (Pause) She is...shapely...this Duncan? Full-breastit?

SEATON. She has apples in her cheeks.

MINISTER. Look out on your own account. Lest it be said you protect her out of lust.

SEATON. You wrong me.

MINISTER. Listen! Are there marigolds on your land?

SEATON. Marigolds?

MINISTER. Marsh...marigolds...on your ploughgate?

SEATON. I fail to——

MINISTER. For each marsh marigold found, the fine is?

SEATON. One sheep.

MINISTER. How much greater penalty, to harbour under your roof-tree a spiritual weed, a festering and infectious growth, a canker.

SEATON. What would you have me do?

MINISTER. See she names names.

SEATON. If she cannot?

MINISTER. She must. To clear her own. There is Justice left in this world, Master. But first, lay bare the Truth. By whatever means you will. For your own good name, as much as hers. Then will the Session take matters into its own scrupulous hands. It is the Lord's work, Master and brings glory!

(Pause)

SEATON. If I fail?

MINISTER. It were better you did not.

Scene 4

(Effie McCalyan's home: the bedroom. Bed, futegang, velvet stool, tapestry, a chamberpot. A table, with FIAN's wares. EFFIE wears an embroidered gown; DR FIAN alias CUNNINGHAM, school-master of Saltpans)

FIAN. This phial contains a secret philtre, comprisit from rare juices of the Orient. I receivit it only after great effort, from a merchant who exchanges local salt for timber, in the German ports. He had it from a sea-captain, a Hollander, whose wares are claimit never to fail. In that he secures substances from Samarkand and beyond. He once had one from snake-juices could kill instant.

EFFIE. This... is not to kill?

FIAN. No, ladyship...this is...for the other.

EFFIE. Is potent?

FIAN. It will bind the recipient to yourself, so long as you please. See...three drops in the evening...either in ale or wine...the latter being less destructive to the desires...nightly upon requirement, till the potion be done.

EFFIE. Nothing else?

34

FIAN. But womanly wiles...

EFFIE. I am in your debt.

FIAN. Never reveal the source. (Pointedly) I am only sorry your ladyship's husband Patrick is abroad these months, that you cannot put it into practice straightway...

EFFIE. (muses) Yes, it will be some time...before I can—

FIAN. You have not heard?

EFFIE. Heard what?

FIAN. (confused) I...that is...

EFFIE. Out with it!

FIAN. It was...our next meeting...the night is almost upon us, and...there are no instructions, as to the addit matter we were to—

EFFIE. How could there be?

FIAN. I had hoped perhaps...he might...the Earl might...

EFFIE. When he is in Tantallon? Stop talking in riddles.

FIAN. The King has had him releasit. Under condition—

EFFIE. When?

FIAN. I have newly—

EFFIE. No, when did the King—?

(Three heavy beats, as with a staff on the ground, off. They freeze, then EFFIE takes FIAN's arm)

This way, quickly... (As she shows him out) Stand by, to be summonit.

(FIAN exits. Pause. BOTHWELL enters, upstage.
Pause, then:)

BOTHWELL. Madam!

EFFIE. My noble Lord!

BOTHWELL. I bring greetings from the Court...to yourself...and your husband...

EFFIE. My husband...is from home...

BOTHWELL. Then our affection...is yours, entire...

EFFIE. I would have it so!

(They eye one another. BOTHWELL bows elaborately.
EFFIE curtseys. Suddenly they drop the pose. She
throws herself into his arms)

How I have missed you.

BOTHWELL. I came as soon as I was releasit.

EFFIE. Maitland did not have you followit?

BOTHWELL. I gave them the slip.

EFFIE. You are quite safe?

BOTHWELL. But for a stiffness in the limbs: a stiffness
that will soon turn...to advantage.

EFFIE. I have told Fian to stand by.

BOTHWELL. The more that congregate in the King's despite,
the more we shall have him in a flurry. It also leaves
us...free to breathe...

EFFIE. It is good to see you again...after these months.

(She puts her arms round his neck)

BOTHWELL. What is this?

(He takes the phial)

EFFIE. Three drops each night, Fian said...rare juices
from the Orient.

BOTHWELL. Rare juices! One part brose, three parts
water of Leith.

EFFIE. You do not trust it?

BOTHWELL. I do not require it.

(He sniffs the phial, pours the contents into the
chamber-pot)

As if we lacked pull in our own bodies, that we should
need philtres and 'rare juices'.

EFFIE. I have criet out for you, in your absence. My body
longs for yours.

BOTHWELL. And mine, for yours...My blood is firit by
your thighs, your warmth, your glow...(He kisses
her, draws her on to the bed) By the magic potion
that runs in your veins...and beats in your breasts...
and makes our bodies one...

(He starts to unclothe her. The lights go down)

Scene 5

(A smithy. Tools of the trade. DAVID SEATON
questions GILLES DUNCAN. THOMAS STRACHAN,
smith, listens)

SEATON. You must tell me, which farm?

GILLES. I have telt you. On the Craigs.

SEATON. Where there was a sick bairn? (She nods) That
    is sick no longer? (She nods) You have curit this
    bairn?

GILLES. I but cradled him in my arms, Master.

SEATON. By whose grace then?

GILLES. By God's good grace, what else?

STRACHAN. (aside) Satan's.

SEATON. How often have you usit this...power, Gilles?

GILLES. I have no power. Had the bairn died, would I
    have been liable?

STRACHAN. Yes!

SEATON. Enough!

STRACHAN. There are tales of sick-making.

GILLES. I have healit only.

STRACHAN. What of the miller's son, that died in the night?

SEATON. It is I who am chargit to put these questions. I
    am instructit by the Minister.

STRACHAN. (spits) The Minister!

GILLES. They say God favours them that love him, and
    obey His commandments.

SEATON. And them that break them? Does God not chastise?

GILLES. (simply) Master, I am in your hands.

SEATON. You must account for...these other nights.
    (Pause) Is there not...some lad?

STRACHAN. (straightens up) What lad would touch her?

When half the village has been up her, afore him?
(As she protests) Look at her, Master...smell her...
she's sticky with it.

GILLES. Not true!

STRACHAN. Bare-facit bitch!

GILLES. He says this, because I preventit him, every time
he wantit me. (Appeals to SEATON) He has tried to
take me, Master...to force me...

STRACHAN. Whoor!

SEATON. I forbid this...wantonness of tongue...Things
must be done...in a seemly fashion...without violence
or abuse...

(He takes GILLES' wrists)

Gilles...you must loose your tongue...else it will be
loosit for you...I speak in your own interest...
What persons have you been with? (As she turns her
head away) Please, Gilles...

(His speech is punctuated by STRACHAN's hammering.
Shouts)

Stop that!

(GILLES has snatched her hands away, pressed them
to her ears. SEATON takes them again)

For your own sake, speak...Gilles...before it is too...

(He turns resignedly to STRACHAN, who steps forward
- a length of rope in his hands. STRACHAN loops the
rope round her forehead. She struggles)

STRACHAN. I'll give her a ...taste of what...her hands,
Master...hold her hands...

(SEATON obeys. STRACHAN tightens the rope.
GILLES screams)

SEATON. Loose the rope! Loose it.

(STRACHAN does so, reluctantly)

That is but a foretaste...of what we must do...if you still refuse.

GILLES. I have nothing...to tell...

STRACHAN. What of Fian?

SEATON. What of him?

STRACHAN. Ask her.

SEATON. Gilles? Fian?

GILLES. Nothing...

(Again they take her. Slowly, rhythmically, the rope eats in)

SEATON. Please, Gilles...please...please...

GILLES. Slacken the rope...my head...my skull...it is being split...in two...

STRACHAN. Fian? Sampson? Napier? No?

(He gives a final twist. She shrieks)

GILLES. Fian! Yes...Fian...yes...yes...yes...

STRACHAN. Sampson?

GILLES. Yes...Agnes Sampson...and Napier...with her...

STRACHAN. And others? Name the others!

GILLES. I will tell you...please...my brain...you bite into...my brain...I will tell you...if...please...

STRACHAN. Agnes Sampson?

GILLES. Midwife...

STRACHAN. (to SEATON) There is always a midwife...

GILLES. Barbara Napier...and others...

STRACHAN. Who else?

GILLES. Janet...Janet Blandilands...and another Agnes,
yes Agnes Thomson...then John Ker...also George
Mott's gudewife, that dwells in Lothian...then the...
the potter's wife at Seaton...

SEATON. Seaton!

STRACHAN. Soon enough for a coven!

GILLES. (incredulous) No! No, we but met...never that,
you never think it was...no...

SEATON. You see the gravity? Who was the prime
mover?

GILLES. I...no, I...there was never any...

STRACHAN. Again?

SEATON. Gilles?

GILLES. (as the smith takes her) Effie...McCalyan...
yes, her...the same whose godfather died...

STRACHAN. She has conspirit?

GILLES. Conspirit!

STRACHAN. Conspirit what?

GILLES. (lost) That she...

(She collapses. STRACHAN dashes water at her)

SEATON. You take over much pleasure in this.

STRACHAN. Every man should take pleasure in his work, Master. The same could turn on you, if the Session wantit.

(The MINISTER appears. He stands silently, watching. GILLES comes round)

Ask her...where do they meet?

SEATON. Where, lass? Where do they meet? Tell us, for your soul's sake...

STRACHAN. (aside) For her white body's sake...

GILLES. Then no more harm will come to me? No more pain? (As he nods his head) None, at all? (But she suddenly shakes her head) No...it is no use...

SEATON. Tranent?

GILLES. Not Tranent...

(STRACHAN sees the MINISTER. The MINISTER makes a slight gesture, so that STRACHAN gives no indication of having seen him)

SEATON. Where, lass...? If not Tranent...?

GILLES. The kirkyard...of North Berwick...

STRACHAN. This is what we have been seeking. They are trappit now, them and their foul horde. That seek pleasure in themselves, and deny it to others...

SEATON. This child, to have been so usit...

GILLES. I may go, now?

SEATON. You may go.

STRACHAN. But——

SEATON. I have been given that assurance. Stand aside.

(STRACHAN glances past SEATON, and receives a
look of approval from the MINISTER. STRACHAN
steps aside. The MINISTER exits, silently)

STRACHAN. I wonder whiles, Master, what goes on under
your roof...Witch that she is!

GILLES. (turning) Good Master...witch is false...witch
is...false...

SEATON. I pray to God it may be.

GILLES. I have your word, Master...you have given me
your word.

SONG. <u>GIFT OF MARIGOLD</u>

Frae the skies cam drizzling rain
On the eard and on the stane
Frae the skies cam sizzling sun
Dries the black eard up again.

Seedlings plantit raw on raw
Turn to stalk and then to straw
Turn to yellow where land was sowed
Each ploughgate a strip of gowd.

I bind marigolds in your hair
Draw them tight and hold them there,
Gift of marigold maks you proud
Of your yellow tresses, rope of gowd.

Binding sunflowers in your hair
Yellow crops, gowd tresses there:
But set them alight and raw on raw
Rats come running frae the straw.

Faster and faster see them come
Each rat trailing a burning plume
Eyes like beads and sizzling skin
See how fast their colours run.

Some will die by stick or stane
Crushed in the black eard one by one,
Others in the ditch or in the pyre
Will die by water or by fire.

Scene 6

(BOTHWELL's house, Leith. A large chest, a table.
BOTHWELL, EFFIE, FIAN. They drink from pewter
mugs, which BOTHWELL refills)

FIAN. (to EFFIE) You have access to a black cat?

EFFIE. I do.

FIAN. Black from snout to tail. Castrate it, and do on it
the marks of thy will. Christen it, then attach to it the
chief parts of a dead man. The joints of the body to be
broken apart and attach it. Then the beast cast into the
full flood. At such time as James sets sail for the
further shore. That he fall utterly. Repeat to me the
instructions for the beast, which you will pass on.

EFFIE. Two of them to hold a finger, one on each side
the chimney-cruik, the two nebbes of their fingers
meeting together. Pass the beast through the links
of the cruik, thereafter under the chimney. Still at
the house, knit the four feet of the beast to the joints
of the dead man. Then fetch it to the shore at
Pittenweem, it being midnight for our cause. Then
cast the burthen into the sea.

FIAN. Your words being?

EFFIE. 'See that there be no deceit among us'.

FIAN. After which the boat should perish. (To BOTHWELL)
To the same end we meet tomorrow.

BOTHWELL. Your task is to vest the image.

(BOTHWELL opens the chest. FIAN brings out
armfuls of garments)

FIAN. Ample...ample...So I may assure them his
Excellency will be there?

BOTHWELL. He will indeed. In true garb. There are
other things, there, you may dispose of at will.

(FIAN eyes the contents of the chest greedily, stuffs
his pouches with what he can: buckles, ornaments,
brooches)

FIAN. This must have a speedy conclusion.

EFFIE. Why must it?

FIAN. They say the Session.has startit to smell out folks'
business.

EFFIE. To what effect?

FIAN. Some servant-lass has been questionit.

BOTHWELL. I have been questionit by the King. It aidit
him little.

EFFIE. Too much is at stake, to call a halt.

FIAN. I hope I may...give your ladyship...every
satisfaction.

BOTHWELL. You will be well rewardit.

(FIAN exits)

EFFIE. (looks up) To cast a dead cat into the sea! To
drown a King! Fian is a schoolmaster, yet deludit

like the rest.

BOTHWELL. James is deludit also. Why should not Fian
claim he can, by his devices, harm the King - when
James himself credits it? Who dare say we are
mistaken, when James attributes storms to black
cats, the scarts on his skin to the scratching of
witches' pins?

EFFIE. Their acts can never be proven.

BOTHWELL. Neither can they be disproven. This is a
strong string to our bow.

EFFIE. If Fian accomplishes what we have set him to do?

BOTHWELL. A triumph. Yet leave us in the clear. No
proof possible. Even if he does not, he still creates
an unease throughout the shires. A confusion, in the
land. Only thus may we change the larger climate of
the times.

EFFIE. Does James suspect?

BOTHWELL. He jumps at his shadow.

EFFIE. Maitland, then? More girth to him?

BOTHWELL. As Chancellor, he is intent on private feuds.
He claims estates for the Crown, to milk them himself.

EFFIE. As my father could testify. Three times Maitland
attemptit to seize our lands. I shall not forgive him,
for what my father went through.

BOTHWELL. Where Maitland keeps a festering stank, I
shall create a lilypond.

EFFIE. The King would destroy your lilypond. And you in
it.

BOTHWELL. He would like to. But he cannot. Because I am his pike. And pike have teeth.

EFFIE. Why not use them?

BOTHWELL. My aim is not self-advancement, but the renewal of the Kingdom.

EFFIE. When James ceases to be King?

BOTHWELL. There will be another.

EFFIE. There will always be Kings?

BOTHWELL. Then there will always be need for you and me, my love...and for dragon's teeth, to sow.

EFFIE. It is you I think of.

BOTHWELL. They are indivisible, what I am and what I am to do.

EFFIE. So are we indivisible...you and I...I am your lilypond...and you...are my pet pike.

(She snaps at him)

BOTHWELL. I hope I may give your ladyship...every satisfaction.

EFFIE. You will be well rewardit.

(EFFIE exits)

BOTHWELL. May she burn like coal, this night...May she burn like coal, as has been ordainit.

(To Black)

SONG. BERWICK-BRIGGE

When the grey howlit has three times hoo'd,
When the grinning cat has three times mew'd,
When the tod has yowl'd three times in the wood,
At the red mune cowerin ahint the cloud,

When the stars hae cruppen deep in the drift,
Lest cantrips had pyked them oot of the lift,
Up horses a', but mair adowe:
Ryde, ryde, for Berwick-Brigge Knowe...

*

Cummer, gae ye afore, cummer gae ye,
Gin ye winna gae, cummer let me,
  Ring-a-ring-a-widdershins,
  Linkin lithely widdershins,
Cummers carline crone and queyn
    Roun gae we:

Cummer gae afore, cummer gae ye,
Gin ye winna gae, cummer let me,
  Ring-a-ring-a-widdershins,
  Loupin lichtly widdershins,
Kiltit coats and fleean hair
    Roun gae we:

Cummer gae ye afore, cummer gae ye,
Gin ye winna gae, cummer let me,
  Ring-a-ring-a-widdershins,
  Whirlin, skirlin widdershins,
And De'il tak the hindmaist
    Whae'er she be!

Scene 7

(North Berwick Kirkyard. Tombstones, trees, candles.
Masked figures. In the background a naked form gyrates
FIAN, in an animal-skin, has a staff in his hand. He
leads them)

48

FIAN. Oh put thy trust in HIM

ALL. We put our trust in HIM

FIAN. That will appear before thee

ALL. That will appear before us

FIAN. And not in God the Father

ALL. Not in God the Father

FIAN. Nor his Son

ALL. Nor His Son

FIAN. Who neither answer

ALL. Who neither answer

FIAN. Nor appear on thy call

ALL. Nor appear on our call

    (FIAN strikes the ground, three times)

FIAN. Benedicite!
               Benedicite!
                        Benedicite!

ALL. Glory!
           Glory!
               Glory!

    (BOTHWELL appears, as the DEVIL: black-masked
and cloaked)

BOTHWELL. I adjure ye, worship only me!

ALL. With full allegiance.

BOTHWELL. My servants shall neither want nor ail anything, nor shall I let a tear drop from their eyes so

long as they serve only me. Now spare not to eat,
drink and be blythe, taking rest and ease. For I
shall raise thee up at the latter day gloriously. Eat
ye...drink ye...

(Moaning, keening from the WOMEN)

ALL.   (FIAN leading)

We eat this meat in the Devil's name
With sorrow and sych and meikle shame
We shall destroy house and hald
Baith sheep and goats intil the fald
Little good shall come to the fore
Of all the rest of this little store.

(He touches them in turn)

(FIAN leading)

And the more to prove our allegiance true
    Like to vassals good and leal
He has brandit our banes wi his Devil's mark
    And our flesh wi his privy seal.

(A wax model of KING JAMES is unveiled)

BOTHWELL.   May winds rise and grow, that they destroy
the false King and Queen.

EFFIE.   Why dost thou bear such a grievance against the
King?

BOTHWELL.   For reason he is the greatest enemy we have
in this world.

FIAN.   Let the King perish.

ALL.   Let the King perish.

(Skewers are thrust into the wax image. BOTHWELL
has gone)

FIAN.   Let King James perish

EFFIE.   Molten by blue fire

AGNES.   And wastit by degrees

FIAN.   Let him perish by water

EFFIE.   By fire

AGNES.   And air

FIAN.   By conjoinment of the elements

EFFIE.   In his despite

FIAN.   By fire and water

ALL.   And fire agen

FIAN.   So let him burn

ALL.   Until Amen

FIAN.   By fire and water

ALL.   And fire agen

FIAN.   So let him burn

ALL.   Until Amen

FIAN   So much for King James the Sixth, ordainit to be
consumit at the instance of a noble man!

(Slow dance. GILLES enters, sees the skewered
image, screams)

Who is she?

AGNES.   Gilles Duncan. From Tranent.

FIAN.   The one that has been interrogatit?

GILLES. Who is that...that man...good Master...I came...

AGNES. That is no man. That's the King.

GILLES. My head...is split...my good Master...

FIAN. I have a mind to silence her.

EFFIE. She's but a silly chicken.

FIAN. She may give away our meeting-place.

EFFIE. We shall soon find another.

GILLES. I have come...to warn you.

(A skewer is held out to her. She thrusts it away, runs. She is stopped in her tracks.)

OFFICER. Stand, in the King's name!

1st SOLDIER. In the name of King James of Scotland, stand!

(SOLDIERS enter, STRACHAN with them. Torches, drawn swords. Panic, milling figures. The wax image is knocked over)

2nd SOLDIER. No you don't, my wee burdie...

OFFICER. (indicates FIAN, still masked) There he is. Our chief prize. He is wantit alive. Do not let him slip!

(FIAN flees, pursued by SOLDIERS. STRACHAN takes GILLES)

STRACHAN. Bite, would you? I'll give you something to bite about.

3rd SOLDIER. Feel like having a go?

STRACHAN. Bloody split her in two!

EFFIE. The lass has done you no harm. Do her none.

OFFICER. So you speak, do you? Superior tones, and all.
Come on, we'll see how you take to a good... plucking...

(As the WOMEN are roped, FIAN is brought in)

So this is the Black Earl, is it? You may worry King
James, sonnie, but you don't fricht me.

FIAN. I am the King's man.

OFFICER. The King of Darkness, belike. You are as
black as the Earl o' Hell's waistcoat. And by God,
you'll pay dear for it. We'll have your marrow
running like candle-wax.

(He tears off FIAN's mask)

FIAN. You are mistaken.

(The OFFICER looks at him, enraged, then strikes
him)

OFFICER. Where... is... Bothwell?

(Silence. As FIAN turns his head away, the OFFICER
clubs him to the ground)

3rd SOLDIER. I kent fine that wasn't Bothwell!

OFFICER. Get a move on. We haven't all bloody night.

(The roped WOMEN are removed. FIAN is dragged
off)

You, bring up the rear.

(He indicates the wax image. 2nd SOLDIER lifts it,
hesitantly)

It's only a bloody doll!

(The SOLDIER exits, with the image. The OFFICER looks round, follows. Only wreaths of smoke remain. BOTHWELL appears. He looks after the SOLDIERS, raises his head, eyes closed)

(Curtain)

ACT TWO

Proclamation

HERALD. When SATAN taks a woman for wife,
She comes to sorrow and meikle strife,
For that her bodie be burnt whole
For good of her immortal soule.

What woman taks SATAN for husbande
Be helde for scorne throughout the land,
And she must drink frae a bitter cup
For fear her soule be rendered up.

Thus hath this present PARLIAMENT
A ledger to the DEVIL sent,
Fully empowred to treat about
Finding revolting WITCHES out.

(Curtain rises)

Scene 1

(Falkland Palace. A courtyard, its centre flags set
out as a chequer-board: red and white squares. The
chequers moved by poles. Birdsong. JAMES and
HOME stand on either side of the board. Extremely
long pause. Ultimately JAMES makes a move. HOME
takes a chequer. JAMES retaliates)

JAMES. Pre...cipi...tate!

HOME. Two can play at that...game...

JAMES. The essence of statecraft: to look as though you
        are headit in the one direction - then loup in the other.

HOME. No-one more adept than your Grace.

JAMES. No news of Maitland? (As HOME shakes his head)
        His transactions in the city take ower long.

HOME. He's scared Edinburgh castle slides into the
        Norloch when he's not looking.

JAMES. He is a trusty Chancellor, for all his foibles.
        And sets good store on the royal coffers. Whereas
        there are some that...line their own pockets...

        (He shoots a look at HOME)

HOME. (coolly) Surely never...prelates exceptit.

JAMES. It has been said...

HOME. Tut tut, your concentration's slippit...

        (This as he takes a chequer)

JAMES. Tut tut tut...

        (As he takes HOME's)

        Not so much a matter of concentration, as of having it
        up here!

        (Taps his head)

HOME. Just so!

        (He takes another)

JAMES. Aye...just so!

        (He retaliates)

HOME. An ambitious piece...that seeks a crown.

JAMES. They are not...easy come by...

(The JESTER enters)

JESTER. Weel playit, Majesty! (To HOME) Is that him
won again?

HOME. We've not finished yet.

JESTER. Best cry it a draw. Here's the rain. (With a
sly look at JAMES) Think there'll be more thunder?

JAMES. (a hand to his ear) Do not mention it.

JESTER. Aw, I forgot...(To HOME) His Majesty can't
stomach the lightning...it brings him out in spots.

JAMES. How about crying it a draw? Time we were in the
saddle.

JESTER. A saddle'll do you little good, if you haven't a
horse.

JAMES. The horse are stablit.

JESTER. (shakes his head slowly) That's what I've come
to tell you. They're gone.

HOME. Gone!

JAMES. If this is a prank, or Nicol hasn't boltit his gates,
we shall——

JESTER. No, it's the horse that's boltit.

HOME. They were lockit in, good and proper.

JAMES. Maybe they broke their tethers...

JESTER. They were untyit.

JAMES. (it dawns) Bothwell! Bothwell has spiritit them away. Praise God our own life has been sparit, through God's mercy.

(JAMES falls to his knees, in thanks)

HOME. Are they all gone?

JESTER. No, just the chestnut and the roan.

HOME. Why did you not say?

JESTER. I couldn't get a word in.

(JAMES is on his feet in a flash)

JAMES. Nothing but the old nags? Scarce fit for tallow. Serve him right! (He tosses his head)

HOME. So we can ride, after all.

JESTER. Unless the deer have been spiritit away by Bothwell.

(JAMES crooks a finger. The JESTER approaches him)

JAMES. You were forbidden our court for thirty days, under pain of a whipping.

JESTER. I'm...a little hard of hearing, Majesty...I didn't...

HOME. Cut off his ears instead. He'd not miss them.

JESTER. (covers his ears) I heard that! (To JAMES) Look, Majesty...you said, if I set foot on the soil of your court...well, this isn't your court. Since you gave it to the Queen, for her wedding...by way of dowry..

JAMES. Man and wife are one. That will not save your hide.

JESTER. Maybe this will'.

> (The JESTER sits on the chequer-board, removes one
> shoe and then the other, and pours sand from them)

'If I set foot on the soil...' I haven't...I've been walking
on Queensferry sand, fresh frae the firth of Forth.

JAMES. Would Papistry take root in't?

JESTER. Tis lustratit by Protestant seas. Am I forgiven?

JAMES. Better than you deserve.

HOME. (puts a finger to his nose.) Put your shoes back
     on, quick...

JESTER. Your nose is too near your arse.

> (The JESTER tries to put on his shoes. JAMES and
> HOME prod him, with their poles. He skips over the
> chequer-pieces. A touch of cruelty in their fun)

HOME. Dance!
          Dance!

JESTER. Help!
           Help!

JAMES. Dance!
          Dance!

JESTER. Aw...naw...

> (The JESTER is on the ground, covering his head.
> SIM and CRAW enter. JAMES and HOME hand the
> poles to them, and exit. SIM and CRAW beat the ground,
> round the JESTER.

Naw...aw...let's cry it a draw, Majestie...

> (From their laughter he realises it is SIM and CRAW.
> He shakes his fist at them. They come forward. The

JESTER puts his shoes on, rubs his bruises)

JESTER. I wish Bothwell <u>had</u> spiritit away the horses.

CRAW. Why?

JESTER. Why do you think?

CRAW. Thinking isn't his line.

JESTER. No more than galloping round the countryside's mine. I've a sore enough backside, as it is.

CRAW. Hear that: he admittit it!

SIM. Admittit what?

CRAW. That he's a pain in the arse.

JESTER. If it comes on buckets, that'll make it even worse.

SIM. It's healthy...keeps you in trim...develops the muscles.

JESTER. What for?

SIM. I'm open to suggestions.

JESTER. Only thing you're open to is ridicule.

CRAW. Depends on your sense of humour. (To SIM, indicating the JESTER) Not that he's got one.

JESTER. Not surprising, the company I keep.

(As they are about to strike him, he drops to his knees, intones:)

Semper ibi oh pudendum
Bonum vinum ad bibendum!

CRAW. What does that mean?

JESTER. A Master of Art
      Is not worth a Fart!

    (Hunting horns loudly, off)

SIM. Come on!

CRAW. We're off!

    (They exit. The JESTER rises)

JESTER. I'm famisht...and I can't stand venison...

    (He exits)

Scene 2

    (Falkland. JAMES's hunting party. JAMES in green
doublet with velvet trimmings; and crimson almost to
the waist. HOME, ATTENDANTS, dabbing themselves
clean. MAITLAND, apart. Also SIM and CRAW.
Hounds)

JAMES. (pettedly) You obstructit the field. Else we had
another stag. Your horse cut across.

HOME. (heatedly) No need to cry off the hounds.

    (The JESTER enters, wearily)

JAMES. There was no scent. Too much rain has made the
dogs' noses dull.

HOME. Too much rain! Kilbuk and Ding-dew are past it!

    (The HERALD enters, wearily)

HERALD. Your Grace...

    (JAMES pays no attention. The HERALD addresses
MAITLAND)

His Grace...

(As he pauses expectantly, the JESTER cuts in:)

JESTER. Has been picking raspberries!

MAITLAND. (to the HERALD) His Grace's physician has ordert him to dip his legs in the belly of a slaughtert stag, to strengthen his sinews.

JESTER. Nae need to go paddlin'.

HERALD. Bothwell has been let slip.

(JAMES and MAITLAND freeze)

JAMES. (in fury) Escapit! Bothwell escapit! Out of your grasp. When you might have had him.

(Pause)

HOME. Was there any doubt he was there?

HERALD. There was——

JAMES. ——no circumstantial doubt. His presence will be confirmit. Who was taken?

HERALD. The most base would appear to be one Cunningham schoolmaster of Saltpans, alias Dr Fian. Whom the Officer mistook for Bothwell.

MAITLAND. And?

HERALD. Sundry women, of varied degree.

MAITLAND. The highest?

HERALD. One Eupham McCalyan.

MAITLAND. Daughter of Lord Cliftonhall. Hence of pedigre We shall see how she takes to interrogation.

HERALD. The charge?

MAITLAND. Witchcraft.

JAMES. A witch is a person that has conference with the
Devil, to take counsel or do some act. For this,
the Devil's bodily presence must be proven. Then
the facts of the conference. Finally, the taking of
counsel, and the act itself.

MAITLAND. Were devices taken?

HERALD. A wax image.

JAMES. What sort of...likeness?

HERALD. Crude.

MAITLAND. In whose possession was it?

HERALD. This Fian.

JAMES. Put him to the test. He appears the major
instrument. The powers of darkness are fell, that
make the royal hand shake. Yet we must defy him.
Till our marriage with Anne bear issue. To maintain
the line. Bothwell is a black stag.

HERALD. And the hinds? What of them?

JAMES. Proven agents must be put to death, in accord with
the laws of God.

HERALD. What manner of death?

JAMES. Kindless. As is commonly usit by fire.

HERALD. Ought then neither sex nor rank to be exemptit?

JAMES. It is the highest point of idolatry, wherein no
exemption is admittet.

HERALD. Bairns not to be sparit?

JAMES. Not a hair the less of my conclusion.

MAITLAND. (impatiently) His Grace condemns all that are of counsel of such crafts.

HERALD. Surely, since this crime be so severely punisht, Judges must beware condemning any, but as are truly guilty?

JAMES. Judges ought indeed. For it is as great a crime - as Solomon hath said - 'to condemn the innocent, as to let the guilty escape free'. Neither ought the report of one infamous person be admittit as sufficient proof, which can stand of no law.

HERALD. What of the guilty confessions that may work against one so accusit?

MAITLAND. The assize must serve for interpreter in that respect.

JAMES. But in our opinion, since in matter of treason against the Prince wives and bairns may serve as sufficient proof, it would seem the more adequate in matters of high treason against God. For who but witches can witness the acts of other witches? Further proof rests in the finding of witches' marks, and also in their fleeting by water. Together with the gushing of blood from the carcass of one destroyit by them. These are God's supernatural signs. Which we interpret as we may.

MAITLAND. They are familiar with the water-test, at Berwick?

HOME. They soon will be.

JAMES. The method straightforward: stripping and binding, then the tying of the thumbs to the toes. (Pause) There is to be an innovation. The right thumb is now to be tied to the left great toe, and vice-versa. Thus making the sign of God's holy cross.

(The JESTER has mimicked the position)

If she sink she be innocent. If she float, guilty - and
treatit according.

HERALD. By what reasoning?

JAMES. Water rejects the flesh of witches, baptisit as
they have been in unholy liquid.

JESTER. In other words, we're a Christian nation!

(As the others turn angrily, he raises an arm)

Full moon and high sea
Shall not touch thee.
Dark dawning, stormy sky,
King James shall never die.

JAMES. It were best not, in that he is God's instrument in
this place, against the lawlessness that shakes loose
the commonweal. It is God's cause, that we are
fighting.

MAITLAND. There are papers to be preparit.

HOME. And apparel to be changit.

JAMES. Only by earnest prayer to God and his Angels of
Light can this disease be curit, and darkness driven
from our shores. The causes are manifest, that
make them rife. For the wickedness of the people on
one hand procures this defection, whereby God punishes
sin, by a greater iniquity. On the other part, the
consummation of the World and our deliverance draw near,
making Satan to rage the more at the imminent o'erthrow
of his instruments. (To HERALD) Prepare a writ, to
have Bothwell declarit outlaw. Have it proclaimit
thrice at the Mercat Cross, and throughout the land.
To this effect: it is for every law-abiding citizen to
apprehend him and bring him to justice, giving respect
neither to him nor his property. Return post-haste,
with notice of our imminent arrival. (To HOME) Let

there be a good meat on the spit, and flagons of red wine. Thereafter we depart for the palace of Holy-roodhouse, and from thence to the Toolbooth. There to stamp the bloody seal upon this affair.

Scene 3

(Tranent. MINISTER and SEATON)

SEATON. You said she would be releasit.

MINISTER. So she was.

SEATON. As bait. For Bothwell.

MINISTER. Who denies King James all dignity.

SEATON. And can look after himself. Which she cannot.

MINISTER. These are confessit witches. They are altogether different.

SEATON. Different?

MINISTER. Defilit.

(Pause)

SEATON. You say...there is no cure?

MINISTER. Only the grave. As for hunchbacks.

SEATON. If I could speak for her.

MINISTER. A great wheel is set in motion, that would crush you.

SEATON. She is innocent.

MINISTER. She has confessit.

SEATON. Under duress.

MINISTER. The Godly remain firm in their resolve. It is Satan's own, that reveal their true colours.

(Pause)

SEATON. What have you...against this Bothwell?

MINISTER. Till he is put down, the King cannot turn his attention to the dissolution of the Popish lords who disdain the true faith.

SEATON. The Kirk's job is to save souls, not abjure them.

MINISTER. Say no more. As for the creature Duncan, her bodily comforts will be seen to, never fear.

SEATON. You...will do nothing?

MINISTER. I will overlook this meeting.

Scene 4

(Bothwell's house, Leith. The HERALD enters)

BOTHWELL. I expectit you sooner.

HERALD. I had to be careful, not to be interceptit. I have come to warn you.

BOTHWELL. Has Maitland turned into the Fox he is?

HERALD. James has had you proclaimit outlaw.

(BOTHWELL turns to face the HERALD)

Your armorial bearings have been torn, at the Mercat Cross.

BOTHWELL. I terrify him so!

HERALD. He blames you, for raising storm.

BOTHWELL. If he catches the croup, he blames me.

HERALD. Soldiers are on their way.

BOTHWELL. Why not sooner?

HERALD. The last place they'd think to find you, is your own hald. There is still time. Head for the Borders.

BOTHWELL. Something I must do, first.

HERALD. You mean...the Lady...

BOTHWELL. Lady?

HERALD. McCalyan.

BOTHWELL. What of her?

HERALD. It is too late...to save her.

BOTHWELL. Why should I save her?

HERALD. I...had heard.

BOTHWELL. Heard what?

HERALD. They say she...has been...seducit.

BOTHWELL. She is a marrit woman. How then, seducit?

HERALD. That she...well...has been led astray...usit.

BOTHWELL. By me?

(The HERALD nods, hesitantly. BOTHWELL pushes him into a chair)

'Led astray...usit...' A mealy mouth, to be a King's

Herald. (He laughs) Bothwell, to seduce...a woman of high degree...daughter of a noble lord...It is kitchen wenches that get themselves seducit...not ladies of style, and pedigree, that wear silks and satins next their skin...Such ladies know best how to...raise the Devil...in a man...how to tempt the flesh...and make it rise...We are not Devils in ourselves, but that women make us so. What is a man to do, but take what is offert him? On a silver platter? Or a paddit couch?

But make no mistake, Herald...it is not Bothwell that seduces...but he who is seducit...time and again, it has been so...Never was Earl so put upon, as this poor fellow that stands before you...whether he wantit it or no, there was little option, no politic escape... this poor woman's tool, that now confronts you...

(As the HERALD rises)

And listen, Herald...when they are done, or undone as you would have it...it is their own look-out...

But you are not a ladies man...I forgot...you are a most moral Herald...and servant of the King...I can tell by your stance you disapprove...a most moral Herald...whose only sin...is to betray his Master...

HERALD. (vehemently) No!

BOTHWELL. He may see it in that light. When you come to the Borders.

HERALD. No.

BOTHWELL. You will not join me?

HERALD. I have a wife, and duties at Court.

BOTHWELL. And set surface glitter against our cause?

HERALD. I am for peace. And always have been. I was not against James, but his excesses. And aimed at

unity, to hold these in check. But each faction has
gone its own gate. While James is grown more mature
in statecraft.

BOTHWELL. In dissimulation.

HERALD. I believe he should retain his throne. And in
due course align it with England's.

BOTHWELL. He still acts in excess.

HERALD. Not to the extent you do. I can no longer stomach
your desperate ways.

BOTHWELL. Who have a wife, and duties at Court! (Pause)
So you side with James, against me.

HERALD. Not against you. Or I would not be here. But
with James, yes. Because he will win through.

BOTHWELL. Why?

HERALD. Because he is the King.

BOTHWELL. And legitimate.

HERALD. That too.

BOTHWELL. But for my impediment, the crown could have
been mine.

HERALD. Or Moray's.

BOTHWELL. They say Moray and the Queen...are at it.

HERALD. I do not know.

BOTHWELL. And if you did, you would not tell! (Pause)
As for McCalyan, you are mistaken. That has nothing
to do with me. Maitland had her taken, because he is
after the lands she inheritit from her father. It is not
his first try.

HERALD. I must go.

> (BOTHWELL holds out his hand. The HERALD takes
> it. BOTHWELL snatches the HERALD's dagger)

BOTHWELL. Is this a plot? A subterfuge? Is some trap
set, between here and the Borders?

HERALD. Not that I know of.

BOTHWELL. Prove your good faith.

HERALD. How?

BOTHWELL. There is a Lady...by whom I would dearly
like...to be seducit!

HERALD. That is no concern of——

BOTHWELL. She has a chamber...in the palace of Holy-
roodhouse...which chamber...has a key.

HERALD. My honour forbids that I——

BOTHWELL. Your honour! That wear one colour on your
front, another to the rear? (Pause, as he toys with
the dagger) James wants me alive? What if Bothwell
were found, with in his breast a dagger...and on its
hilt, the initials of the King's Herald? Or in the
breast of some other...convenient corpse? (Pause)
The Lady Atholl...has a chamber...in Holyroodhouse..

HERALD. No!

BOTHWELL. When the key to that chamber...rests in this
palm this dagger will be returnit to the King's Herald...
who has his wife...and duties, at Court.

> (Pause)

HERALD. You revolt me! You are...a bee at a honeycomb.

BOTHWELL. You disapprove?

HERALD. I merely wonder at it.

BOTHWELL. What wonder you? I shall give you occasion
to wonder!

(BOTHWELL raises the dagger. He seems about to
stab the HERALD. Instead he plunges it into his own
belly. He falls to the ground, with a howl. The
HERALD stands petrified. At last he stoops to touch
BOTHWELL. BOTHWELL squirms aside and rises
to his feet, laughing. He holds out the dagger)

BOTHWELL. Here...take it!

(The HERALD takes the dagger. He exits, without
speaking. BOTHWELL looks after him)

Such sleekit pawns...are needit...in the game we
play...

(Suddenly:)

McCalyan! What is McCalyan...to me? Nothing!
She is past...and done with...It cannot be...otherwise..
But must...be so...Past...and no more...to me...
or anything...in this stinking pit of a world...this
rotten cell...where kings smile...and strut...

(His tone changes:)

God help her...God help them all...for no-one else
will...

SONG.   THE BADGER'S FUR...

The badger's fur is black and white
I make a money purse out of it.

Wild boar has a bristly pelt
Slice it into a yellow belt.

72

Russet-coloured fox is fine
Ladies like him next their skin.

In winter tak the weasel and stoat
Turn them into an ermine coat.

The beardit buck upon the brae
Will come upon an evil day:

They will be catcht in subtle traps
Ladies will wear them on their laps.

Not even the lavrock will escape
Whose feathers deck a nobleman's cape.

However sweetly she has sung
The philomel will lose her tongue.

Lion's the one we all adore
In one hand water, in one hand fire.

Yet see him put his head atween his knees
And pass the time scratching for fleas.

Scene 5

(The Tolbooth. McCalyan's Trial. The Indictment.
Effie, centre-stage, in a white shift, her hair shorn,
ankles tied. The OFFICER by her. JAMES plays
nervously. With him, the HERALD and HOME, the
latter with a flippant air. MAITLAND as Interlocutor.
JUDGE, DEMPSTER, SCRIVENER, SOLDIERS, others.
The MINISTER and SEATON)

DEMPSTER. (reads) '...indictit of bewitching by your airt
of Sorcery, John Johnston, Miller's son of Tranent,
being of 17 yrs of age, by the which witchcraft he died;
and thereby for the cruel slaughter and murder of him;

Item the twelfth, indictit with consulting with Agnes

Sampson aforesaid and ither divers witches for the treasonable staying of the Queen's homecoming by raising storm and wind, to that effect, or else the drowning of her Majestie and her company by conjuring of catts and casting them in the sea at Leith, at the back of Begie-Todd's house, also criet Rbt Grierson;

And generally you are indictit for common witch, having usit'and practisit these sorceries and witchcrafts, divinations and charms, as is particular above-written, and giving yourself furth to have such knowledge, to the abuse of the people. And to the detriment of the King's Majestie within his Realm - in the furthering of the work of the Devil your Master. And ought to be judgit to death thereof and in dry exemplar to ithers to do the like'.

Here endeth the indictment.

(The scroll is handed to the JUDGE. JAMES beckons for it, glances at it, and returns his attention to EFFIE. MAITLAND bows to JAMES, and to the JUDGE)

The Interrogation

MAITLAND. Have you ever intendit the death of the King?

EFFIE. Never.

MAITLAND. You have had no illicit liaison, to put this into practice?

EFFIE. Never.

MAITLAND. You would renounce all such claims against you?

EFFIE. I would truly.

MAITLAND. What of Gilles Duncan, servant to David Seaton, Depute-Bailiff of Tranent, of this Kingdom?

EFFIE. I have never met Seaton.

JAMES. Satan, more like.

MAITLAND. What of Agnes Sampson?

EFFIE. I have no business with her.

MAITLAND. She has had business with you. She has
confessit taking a black toad, hanging it by the heels
three days to let the venom drip out, that she collectit
the venom in an oyster-shell, till she could find a
piece of linen cloth belonging to his Grace, which she
would obtain by the service of one John Ker, an
attendant in his Majesty's chamber. This same Ker
refusit to help her, and reportit the same.

JUDGE. To the saving of his soul.

MAITLAND. The said Agnes further confessit that, had she
obtainit any single piece of linen cloth worn by the
King, she would have bewitched him instant to deathh
by extraordinary pains, as if he had lain among thorns.
You had no part in this? Or in taking a tom-cat
christent with ceremony, thereafter conveying the
beast into the sea?

EFFIE. You wrong me.

MAITLAND. This done, there arose great storm. Causing
the foundering of a boat bound from Bruntisland to
Leith.

JUDGE. True or false?

EFFIE. False.

MAITLAND. Sampson said false. Till she was strippit,
and the Devil's mark found on her privates. She did
straightway confess.

EFFIE. I am an honest woman.

MAITLAND. Greymeal?

EFFIE. Greymeal?

MAITLAND. Barbara Napier?

EFFIE. You have found nothing against her.

JUDGE. Not yet.

MAITLAND. It is further statit you did dance in the kirkyard of North Berwick. The major aim being to harm
your King.

EFFIE. Cannot friends meet, for simple pleasure?

MAITLAND. Simple pleasure? To destroy a King? By
conspiracy?

EFFIE. Conspiracy travels on tiptoe, a finger to its mouth.
Not openly with song and dance.

MAITLAND. You were in the abandonment of your lusts.

EFFIE. We were all women.

MAITLAND. Fian was there. Who has been since broken
on the rack.

EFFIE. I did not see him.

MAITLAND. He did not incite you against the King?

EFFIE. Why should he, as a leal subject?

JUDGE. You answer questions, not put them.

MAITLAND. You were their leader?

EFFIE. No.

MAITLAND. Intermediary then? Between them and the
Unknown? You deny it?

EFFIE. How can I deny what is unknown?

MAITLAND. You confirm, then?

EFFIE. I did not say so.

MAITLAND. Gilles Duncan was of your company?

EFFIE. No, she... she is but a lass, and of no significance.

(MAITLAND looks up at the JUDGE)

JUDGE. Bring Duncan.

(GILLES is dragged into Court, shorn and bound. She falls to the ground. HOME sniggers)

MAITLAND. Gilles, tell us once more... of that night at Berwick-Brigge. When you were with the others... His Grace would be glad to—

GILLES. Grace... I beg for Grace... my lord...

EFFIE. Leave her in peace. She is innocent of—

MAITLAND. Innocent? After your foul play? Your singing and jigging...

GILLES. Ring-a-ring-a-widdershins... round gae we... Linkin blithely... to the sweet... the sweet...

MAITLAND. Were you one of them, Gilles?

GILLES. No... never one... my lord... my good Master... never one...

EFFIE. There is your answer.

MAITLAND. But you were going to be, is that not right, Gilles? Soon?

GILLES. Soon, they were... going to receive me... into their arms... and let me lie there... please... only sleep...

MAITLAND. (close to her) Who was going to receive you?

GILLES. Effie...with all her riches...the kindest...my lady...

JUDGE. To what end? Were they going to receive you?

MAITLAND. Tell us, and then you may sleep.

GILLES. That I may...sleep...sound... (She looks up suddenly) Why, they were going to make me a witch!

(Sudden blackout)

The Interrogation (contd)

MAITLAND. I put this to you. That you were not merely witch, in attempt to smear others; but yourself actit in accord. In devising means of harming his Grace. That his body waste away, his image be consumit by flame, that he be in agony thereby.

EFFIE. His Grace looks fit enough.

MAITLAND. Not through your efforts, but in their despite. Do you recall these rites? (As she shakes her head) I shall refresh your memory.

(A cover is removed from the wax image)

EFFIE. It is little like the King, to me.

JUDGE. Such remarks do not improve the standing of the Panel.

MAITLAND. There is further evidence that certain pins, removit from that effigy, had been seen at your home. Pins of silver, and gold. In keeping with your station.

EFFIE. A costly pastime.

MAITLAND. Yet cheap, to do away with a King.

(He is handed down pins, by the DEMPSTER)

EFFIE. You cannot catch me on that score.

MAITLAND. (to EFFIE) You have never seen these pins
before?

(They are held before her)

EFFIE. Never.

MAITLAND. Bring in Duncan.

EFFIE. This is kindless. How can she——?

OFFICER. Shut your mouth.

(GILLES is dragged in. She is shown the pins)

MAITLAND. Tell us, where have you seen these before?
Whose are they?

GILLES. The dew is like diamonds...on the grass...these
are...such fine...my Lady...

MAITLAND. You have nothing to fear, on her account.

GILLES. I have seen them...

MAITLAND. In a home?

GILLES. In the home...of Effie McCalyan...there...she
is a fine Lady...

EFFIE. This child has never been to my house.

JUDGE. Do not interrupt.

MAITLAND. How else have you seen these pins usit?

GILLES. She had such lovely...tresses...so like a Lady...
of noble birth...

79

MAITLAND. Where else, Gilles?

GILLES. They were...stickit in that man there.

MAITLAND. What did you stick pins in him for?

GILLES. Never I...what would a good lass do the likes of
that...I was busy, besides...

MAITLAND. Busy?

GILLES. I was playing my tune...my Lord...

(JAMES has leaned forward, cupping an ear so as to
make out what she is saying)

JAMES. Was there an instrument? With her?

MAITLAND. There was.

(MAITLAND lifts a jew's harp. JAMES steps forward,
takes it gingerly. He gives it to GILLES, encourages
her)

JAMES. Let her...give us...here you are...lass...play
on it, to your heart's content...

(She plays. JAMES is enraptured)

MAITLAND. The womenfolk jigging the while...this to
provide the beat...so she says...

(JAMES claps his hands)

EFFIE. A drear tune, to jig to.

(A Voice from the back of the Court: SEATON)

SEATON. Your Majesty.

JUDGE. Silence!

JAMES. Let him speak.

80

SEATON. Stop her.

(SEATON comes forward)

JAMES. This may well be her last tune on earth. Would you deprive her of it?

SEATON. I protest. She is not acquaint with the—

EFFIE. Never fear Master, she does not sense it. They have already done their work on her.

JUDGE. Your name, Master?

SEATON. David Seaton, my Lord.

MAITLAND. (to JAMES) The depute-bailiff. From Tranent.

SEATON. I am her Master, Sire. I must...protest at this treatment of her...

JUDGE. Her treatment is in keeping with her sins.

SEATON. Spare some pity for her in her distress.

JAMES. Pity a witch!

SEATON. I beg she be sparit. Instead of what...you have in store.

JUDGE. We would save her soul.

SEATON. She cannot defend herself.

JUDGE. Tell us Master, do you plead for all, or only this one?

SEATON. She is the only one, my Lord. The only one I'd defend.

JUDGE. Defence amounts to defiance.

SEATON. Intercede, then.

JAMES. A witch must have no-one in this world.

SEATON. She is no witch. I swear it.

JUDGE. Can you prove it? At law?

SEATON. She has been a constant comfort to the sick. Not even the Minister could deny she—

JAMES. 'Satan can transform himself into an Angell of Light': Second Corinthians, eleven and fourteen.

SEATON. Say... some folly came over her... for a spell...

JAMES. As Christ says, 'It is not anything that enters in that defiles, but only that which precedeth and cometh out.'

SEATON. I speak out of no disrespect to your Grace... or towards this assize... but because....

(He is lost for words)

Let her return to Tranent. I shall answer for her. And act as surety, however the Court command... keeping a careful eye... on her behaviour.

(He looks up)

The Minister there... can supervise... in matters of...

(But the MINISTER stiffens, turns his head away)

My Lord... we have walls to big, ditches to be dug... but there is also women's work... fruit to pick, cream to skim, water to be drawn from the well... These tasks she can fulfil... the stitching of garments... and much else besides...

(He appeals)

My Lord... Please...

JUDGE. Enough of your prattle.

SEATON. I see no logic, in her suffering.

JAMES. If an arm offend thee, cut if off. If an eye, cut it out. That the remainder of the body be whole. There is logic. Not logic mere, but Logos, the Word. Would you give free rein to them that would tear down God's Kingdom?

(GILLES starts to strum on the harp)

SEATON. Gilles...Gilles...

MAITLAND. Do you not see, she does not know you.

SEATON. Gilles, lass...

JUDGE. We await your decision.

SEATON. I am torn...

MAITLAND. And may well be.

EFFIE. (to SEATON) It is too late, Master...

SEATON. (after a pause) Forgive me...I wish to God I had more courage...

(SEATON exits. At a sign from HOME, two soldiers follow. GILLES plays the jew's harp)

MAITLAND. Courage enough... (To GILLES) One thing more, then that is all. Who was it, led the circle round the image?

JUDGE. She has said, the Panel.

MAITLAND. Then what was said, Gilles? What did they say?

GILLES. They said...the blackthorn and the may...the laverock and the merle...the coushat and the philomel...

all on a sweet summer's day...the fulmart and the
fox...with busy bears and brocks...did...all did
together...did together...play...

MAITLAND. (gently) Can you remember? Tell his
Grace...and he will be well pleasit.

GILLES. I would always please his Grace...my gracious
Master...has gone...

MAITLAND. Yes.

GILLES. I am all alone.

MAITLAND. We are with you. Was it...about King James
the Sixth?

GILLES. Yes...that is right...they said...

JUDGE. Speak up, child.

GILLES. 'This is James the Sixth, orderit to be consumit
at the instance of a noble man.'

MAITLAND. What noble man?

GILLES. Of breeding...the highest...

MAITLAND. Fian?

GILLES. Higher...

MAITLAND. Did you see him?

GILLES. The once.

MAITLAND. Was he dark, or fair?

GILLES. Fair.

JUDGE. Not Fian. The...Other...

GILLES. Oh...dark...

MAITLAND. Did you touch him?

GILLES. No. But he touchit me.

MAITLAND. Was he...hot? Or cold?

GILLES. He came, and causit all the company to kiss his
hinder parts...which were...as cauld as ice...His
body as hard as iron...his face terrible, his nose the
beak of an eagle, great burning eyes...that did leme
of licht...claws to his hands...his feet...hairy...
like a griphon...

JAMES. (sotto) Hepburn is hirsute.

MAITLAND. His voice?

GILLES. Was soft...low and soft...like the wind in the
corn...at twilight...but so cold...so cold...like the
time in the mill-stream...when I fell in, as a child...
under the ice...

MAITLAND. He kisst you?

GILLES. I cannot recall...whether he...he kissit me...
he kissit...he kissit me...and his body was cauld,
but oh his kiss was warm...like blood...on my lips...
                    Have I done well, my lord?

MAITLAND. Did he give himself a name?

GILLES. I scarce remember...it was soon morning...the
world full of throstles...a dewy cage...

MAITLAND. What was his name?

GILLES. The...the Earl...the Black Earl...but it was
others that he kissit, my lord...I am a good girl...
a good girl, Master...in my dewy cage...of grass...

(Sudden Blackout. A spot, for:)

SONG.   THAT SHE WAS A WITCH

That she was a witch, that she was a witch,
   They had nae shadow of doubt,
They prickit her body frae head tae heel
   To find the witch-mark out.

That he was a witch, that he was a witch,
   They had nae shadow of doubt,
So they gave him the rack, they gave him the screw
   And then they gave him the boot.

That she was a witch, that she was a witch,
   There was nae shadow of doubt,
So they gave her the test, the water test,
   And then they fishit her out.

That they were all witches, that they were all
                                        witches,
   Was took for grantit quite,
So they strung them up wi' tarry ropes -
   And then they bade them goodnight...

The Interrogation (contd)

EFFIE. Why must the answer always be witchcraft? To
        anything that frights you? When Bothwell was chasit
        to the Tyne, your Grace's horse was seen to stumble.
        Your Grace was heard to cry out, 'Witchcraft!' That
        was not witchcraft!

MAITLAND. What then?

JAMES. (to SCRIVENER) Note this.

EFFIE. A rabbit hole.

MAITLAND. The ways of witches can be simple. Crude,
        as well as complex. This Fian has been seen flying
        through the air. Over walls and biggins. No horse
        near.

86

EFFIE. Many's the man sees his companions fleeing, at
      night. And forgets it next morning, when he's sobert
      up.

MAITLAND. Yet things exist in the land, to do evil.

EFFIE. They say there are black bogles in Loch Morar,
      that blow out steam, and eat men.

JAMES. (to SCRIVENER) Register that.

MAITLAND. You are happy in this land?

EFFIE. Happy?

MAITLAND. These things and persons we speak of, are an
      attempt to o'erthrow Law and Order. To do away with
      true Government, that Another may rule in its stead.
      Letting the Government, as has been said, go to the
      Devil.

EFFIE. I suspect it is there already, from the misery
      around.

MAITLAND. You have an interest in Government?

EFFIE. Not I.

MAITLAND. But your Master has.

EFFIE. My Master?

MAITLAND. Bothwell.

EFFIE. He is not my Master.

MAITLAND. Help us trap him, you will earn the King's
      lasting pleasure.

EFFIE. I have heard the King's pleasure is seldom lasting.

MAITLAND. Bothwell has assuredly led you in unholy
      worship.

EFFIE. Led who?

MAITLAND. Those we have spoken of. Fian, and Sampson, and—

EFFIE. Whom you torture, for your own satisfaction. You dream up devils, so that you can put them down. What purpose does such cruelty serve? Or is it because we are Catholics, that we are treatit so?

MAITLAND. Not because you are Catholics. But to show our Kirk is as vigilant as yours, in its zeal against the powers of Darkness.

(JAMES signs to MAITLAND. They whisper together. MAITLAND resumes his stance. JAMES is attentive)

You know the penalty for Treason? And that it is Treason to support a rebel? An outlaw, against the throne?

EFFIE. (wearily) Yes.

MAITLAND. You still say Bothwell is nothing to you?

EFFIE. How could he be?

MAITLAND. Then he is without a friend in this land. His proper place is in the Tolbooth. But he has a hide-out. The court would favour anyone...that would reveal that hide-out.

EFFIE. You needn't try to bargain with me.

MAITLAND. You protect him still?

EFFIE. I am exhaustit.

MAITLAND. You protect him, at your peril.

EFFIE. We have been over this.

MAITLAND. And must continue to do so.

EFFIE. I am in no position to—

MAITLAND. It is treason to protect a traitor.

EFFIE. Will this business soon be——?

MAITLAND. Bothwell is a traitor.

EFFIE. Why 'Bothwell' me?

MAITLAND. He is nothing to you?

EFFIE. Nothing.

MAITLAND. Nor you to him?

EFFIE. Nor I to him.

MAITLAND. That I accept. (Pause) Or he would be here, to protect you.

JAMES. He would have appearit—

MAITLAND. —on a shining stallion—

JAMES —at the head of a glittering troop—

MAITLAND. —and made a triumphal exit—

JAMES. —whereas he has gone to ground—

MAITLAND. —to save his skin—

JAMES. —at the expense of yours—

MAITLAND. —which he would not have done—

JAMES. —had you meant the least thing to him.

EFFIE. You toy with me!

JAMES. We shall tell you why he has not come. Because he lies with his whoors. In a secret bed. Under a greasy coverlet, arm in arm.

EFFIE. This is obscene.

JAMES. Not so obscene as their posture. You cannot bear the thought, who bear his seal upon your privy parts.

EFFIE. I have never lain with him.

JAMES. Others have! His presence has been notit. And provit. He leaves a mark on a woman. Between her thighs. Like a great fish, with silver scales.

EFFIE. Please...

JAMES. We see it, before our eyes. Bothwell taking these filthy creatures, baring their flesh, thrusting their legs apart...then doing his will.

EFFIE. No!

JAMES. One after another on beds of straw...beneath his embrace...or lying on velvet, like liquid gold...

EFFIE. Never!

JAMES. Can you not imagine? Do you not envy them? Think of it! Your flesh, one with his. As he prises your body, and takes his fill...Bothwell on top, yourself working below...panting and huffing, his body making its mark...breath fiery, as he splits you... your breasts like petals, beneath his thrust... opening to him...love swelling and rising...limbs entwinit and threshing...his seed spilling, your juices commingling...soft flesh worked to a frenzy, as he rides you and rides you...festooned in your lust!

(She shrieks, tries to cover her ears)

You! And Bothwell your Master!

EFFIE. I have no Master.

90

JAMES. Every woman has a Master.

EFFIE. Not Bothwell.

JAMES. He has ridden you.

EFFIE. No!

MAITLAND. Not Bothwell?

EFFIE. Not Bothwell.

MAITLAND. Whom, then?

EFFIE. Whomsoever you wish.

MAITLAND. The Black Devil himself!

EFFIE. The Black Devil himself...if you would have it so...

    (She is reeling)

JAMES. 'Thou shalt not suffer a witch to live!'

MAITLAND. Not treason. But sorcery. In professit
    presence of Satan, her hideous Master.

JAMES. We have taken not Bothwell, but an Other.

EFFIE. This is a trick...your subtle words...and images...
    have upset my senses...

MAITLAND. You are deliverit up in accordance with God's
    will. I call the indictment proven.

    (EFFIE collapses. JAMES faces the Court)

JAMES. This corruption here, bairns suck at the pap. Our
    conscience doth set us clear in this instance, as did
    the conscience of Samuel - that did say unto Saul:
    'that disobedience is as the sinne of witchcraft': to
    compare to a thing that were not, were too absurd.

So as we have begun, we plan to go forward. Not
because we are James Stewart, and can command so
many thousands of men - but because God hath made
us King and Judge, to make righteous judgment.

Witchcraft, a crime known to be common amongst us,
we call an abominable sin, and that most odious:
<u>Maleficium</u> or <u>Veneficium</u> - an ill or poisonable deed.

We have spent three quarters of a year sifting out
those that are guilty of the same. And by God's
law punishable by death. For them that are found
guilty, they must be rendert up in accord with the
law.

And so demand a verdict in this case.

The Verdict

(EFFIE dragged upright)

JUDGE. We find dealings with the Devil, and the Devil's
bodily presence, proven. Second, full conference
with the Devil, proven. Finally, the taking of council
and study of the act itself, proven. That being the
true verdict of this Court.

(To EFFIE) This day, Eupham McCalyan, spouse to
Patrick Moscrop, alias McCalyan, being presentit
here on Panel, as she that was convictit in Court of
Justiciary here held in Edinborough the 15th day of
June, 1591; and in view and due consideration of the
articles heretofore indictit and read, and on her own
confession before the Court and in presence of his
Grace, is hereby given to sentence, by the mouth of
Wm Grey, Dempster:

(All rise)

DEMPSTER. 'That the said EUPHAM McCALYAN, as

culpable and guilty thereof, be taken to the Castel-
Hill of Edinborough, and there—

EFFIE. Not stranglit...never stranglit...

OFFICER. Shut your mouth.

DEMPSTER. —The Castel-Hill of Edinborough, and there
bound to a stake and burnt alive to ashes. And all her
lands, steadings, heritages and cattle to be forfeit.
Which I, Dempster to this Court, do hereby give for
doom.'

EFFIE. Sweet Christ...to be burnt alive...never to be...
have pity on a poor child in Christ...sweet Jesu, have
pity...

JAMES. There can be no appeal. It is not we that do this
thing, but Christ God; in that we are the Lord's anointit,
and true servant and child of God, while thou art a
vessel of His wrath.

EFFIE. He will save me...he will rescue me...never fear...

JAMES. Thus perish all Infidels!

EFFIE. No...you will never...I defy you...I defy you, to
the uttermaist, and your vicious ways...I glory in it...
I glory...glory...glory...

(EFFIE, arms outstretched, is removed bodily by the
OFFICER. Blackout)

SONG.   THE BURNING

They trailed her to the high Castel-Yett
   And hemmed her about,
And they smeared her ower frae head tae heel
   To drive the witch-mark out.

They harled her to the Castel-Court,
    And smeared her ower wi tar,
And they chained her to an iron bolt
    An eke an iron bar.

They biggit a pile aboot her bodie
    Twa Scots ells up and higher
Then the hangman cam, wi a lowin torch,
    And kindelt the horrid pyre.

Flames met and broke, in seikly smoke,
    A red ball in the sky;
And then it turned, and then it fell
    To ashes suddenly.

The King transfixt in wonder stood
    And scarce believed his e'en,
And all aghast the courtiers cowerd
    As spell-bound they had been.

But that ae night, his Majestie
    As in his bed he lay

(Last couplet spoken)

Did find his thochts did wander to
    Anither Judgment Day...

Scene 6

(JAMES's bedchamber, Holyrood. A carved four poster.
Early morning. JAMES snores. Slight sounds,
whispers, off. A break in the rhythm of the snoring.
A gleam in the shadows. JAMES stirs in his sleep.
Suddenly he sits bolt upright, rubs his eyes. BOTHWELL
emerges from the shadows, with a drawn sword)

JAMES. (screams) Treason...Treason...

(BOTHWELL approaches the bed)

Help! Help!

BOTHWELL. No-one will answer.

JAMES. The Guard? My gentlemen of the bed-chamber?

BOTHWELL. Taken care of.

JAMES. How...how did you...? Treason!

(BOTHWELL throws a key on the bed)

We shall have you hangit!

(BOTHWELL plucks the bed-clothes with the sword.
JAMES shrinks back, then leaps out of bed: ungainly
in cap and nightshirt. BOTHWELL in black, JAMES
in white)

BOTHWELL. Who'll do the hanging? When the King's on
the floor of his chamber, a sword through his——

JAMES. (cringes, wrings his hands) So...after all your
intrigues...and affairs...it is come to this...to play
assassin...by moonlight...to soil your hands, with...
(He challenges) Did your covens not work? (No reply)
Aaaah...that's why you're...to avenge them, is it?
Aaaaah...It'd have done...them more good, if you'd
come to treat for them...while they were still alive.

BOTHWELL. Why should I do that?

JAMES. You were guilty of their deaths.

BOTHWELL. No more than you, who passed sentence on
them, and had them executit.

JAMES. You are a force for evil. I for good.

BOTHWELL. You delude yourself. You call evil, what it
suits you to call evil. There is no such thing as black
and white, in these matters.

JAMES. Through you, they treatit with the Devil. Were made contaminate.

BOTHWELL. All that concerns you is policy...and your own preservation.

JAMES. They were consignit to the flames, by God's Law.

BOTHWELL. Do you not have them on your conscience?

(JAMES on the bed)

JAMES. You should have been there. To hear their cries, as the flames lickit at their feet. To hear her scream, and beg for Grace. Yet refuse to confess out of lealty to you. To the peril of her soul. Can you see her, at the stake? Atoning for what you made her do? Can you not feel for her? Feel the flesh burn, the fats sizzle and cinder, as the faggots fume? Her lush muscles shrink, sinew shrivel and crack? Her parts of womanhood——

BOTHWELL. She was a lamb let to the slaughter.

JAMES. Through you!

BOTHWELL. Through you!

JAMES. (holds up a Bible) 'Put on the whole armour of God, that ye may be able to stand the wiles of the Devil' - Ephesians six and eleven.

BOTHWELL. (strikes the Bible with his sword) You're pretty nakit at the moment.

JAMES. I worship the Lord God of Hosts. While I have heard. your minions make obeissance...in a ritual...one degree more obscene than the kissing of the Papal great toe.

BOTHWELL. It is no great matter which God we worship. The world remains a parchit place.

JAMES. By your pestilence.

BOTHWELL. When there should be more in it to admire
than despise.

JAMES. Pestilence is to be despisit. And burnt out.

BOTHWELL. To burn houses will not destroy the plague.

JAMES. That will be arrivit at.

BOTHWELL. Root out one pestilence, you make room for
another. And end, never seeing the truth.

(JAMES goes to BOTHWELL)

JAMES. We are the Truth. You do Devil's work. And are
now come to seek your King's life. I am wholly in
your power. Better die with honour, than live in
shame. I am ready to die. Take my miserable life.
But before God, I swear thou shalt not have my soul.

(JAMES bares his chest, closes his eyes. Instead of
striking, BOTHWELL kneels at JAMES's feet. JAMES
opens one eye)

Kneel not, adding hypocrisy to treason. Is the manner
of your entrance that of a suppliant? I am no longer
a boy or a minor, to be treatit as a fool. You, Francis
Hepburn, have plottit my death. I call on you, dis-
charge your dishonourable purpose. I will not live a
prisoner, and dishonoured. I am ready!

(But BOTHWELL kisses his sword, renders it up)

BOTHWELL. I harbour no ill-will toward your person. You
are my sovereign, and I your subject.

JAMES. Then what on earth...is it you...? (He scratches)

BOTHWELL. Stop playing with yourself!

JAMES. (a scream) What is it you want?

BOTHWELL. Annulment of outlawry. Repeal of the edict

against me. Full remission of all bygane offences, and restoration of offices, properties and titles; the same to be ratifiet by Parliament at Linlithgow. Your word to act as surety meantime.

JAMES. Is that all?

BOTHWELL. That is all.

JAMES. What makes you think...

(He breaks off, clenches his fists. He controls himself)

If I were to refuse?

BOTHWELL. In that courtyard are three hundred men from the Borders. If by dawn, they have not had the signal, they take this palace and put everyone in it to the sword.

JAMES. The signal?

BOTHWELL. From you. 'God save King James of Scotland, and his belovit cousin the Earl of Bothwell!'

JAMES. Three hundred...

BOTHWELL. Oh, I forgot. There is one other thing. My position at Court.

JAMES. Was forfeit.

BOTHWELL. I would like it back.

JAMES. You belong in a dungeon.

BOTHWELL. You had me releasit.

JAMES. But Maitland...he would never consider...it is too much for...

(JAMES is distraught)

BOTHWELL. Maitland can go.

JAMES. He is my Chancellor.

BOTHWELL. Find another. I want him removit. It is a
small price to pay. For life and liberty.

JAMES. You have no right!

BOTHWELL. You see yourself as the one and only true power.
Absolute. And any force opposing you, not power but
violation of power. Mere violence. In time to come
you will realise you are but an infringer of power. Already there are movements afoot. To make rulers act
in accord with the will of their people, not their own whim.

JAMES. That would be chaos. Men must be governed.

BOTHWELL. So must monarchs. That men may be free in
themselves.

JAMES. Who are you, to think yourself so superior?

BOTHWELL. Your dark shadow, whom you cannot go without.

JAMES. I say you are in league with the Devil.

BOTHWELL. There are many Devils, cousin.

JAMES. I mean Satan.

BOTHWELL. I know his haunt.

JAMES. (approaches him) Tell me. That I may burn him out.

BOTHWELL. He is in this chamber.

JAMES. Where, in this chamber?

BOTHWELL. Why here, cousin...

(BOTHWELL taps himself on the chest. JAMES
gapes)

99

JAMES. You...openly confess it!

BOTHWELL. And here...

> (Touching JAMES lightly on the chest)

> ...as much as anywhere.

> (JAMES is speechless, hand on heart)

> You seem to recognise his haunt at last.

> (Pause)

> We are the upper and nether millstones, you and I.
> One way or another, it is those trappt in the middle,
> must pay the price.

JAMES. (indicating BOTHWELL's sword) And this?

BOTHWELL. The King's. If he will have it.

JAMES. Sheathe it.

> (BOTHWELL does so)

BOTHWELL. But remember, my dearie...one day will
come the time of the real burning! (pause) It is
almost light.

> (BOTHWELL supports JAMES as he crossed slowly
> and unsteadily)

JAMES. (calls, off) Long live King James! And his cousin..
And...his...belovit cousin...the Earl of Bothwell...

> (A great cheer, off. BOTHWELL exits. Pause.
> JAMES appears, looks round. He is overcome. He
> crosses to the bed, kneels by it. A single spot on him)

> I trowe in Almychte   God that wrochte
> Baith in Heavin and Eard   and all of nochte;
> And to His dear Sonne   Jesu Christe,

Was gotten of   the Haly Ghaist.
He bade us come   and there to doom
Baith quick and dead   to His Kingdome.
O keep me frae   the felon slae.
Thou, Lord, for Thy   bitter Passioun
Keep me frae Sinne   and warldly Shame,
And endless Damnatioun.

Grant me the Joye   never will be gane
For sweete Jesu's sake...

                              Amen.

(The town bell has started to toll. The spot on
JAMES dims, slowly)

(Curtain)

THE SCOTTISH LIBRARY

This important series of books of Scottish interest, containing classics and modern titles, and including all the big names of the Scottish literary tradition, is suitable for both academic use and general reading. The distinguished panel of editors includes those working in the literature departments of the principal Scottish universities. The general editor is Alexander Scott of the Department of Scottish History and Literature at Glasgow University.

CONTEMPORARY SCOTTISH VERSE
Edited by Alexander Scott and Norman MacCaig

Two hundred and forty poems by modern Scottish poets, ranging from Hugh Mac Diarmid (b. 1892) to Alan Bold (b. 1943)   £1.75*, 75p+

JAMIE THE SAXT
A Play by Robert McLellan
Edited and annotated by Ian Campbell and Ronald D.S. Jack

Written in authentic Scots, this play presents a portrait of a remarkable king under stress, recreating with that special skill which is Mr. McLellan's hallmark the life of the middle classes and the royalty of the old town of Edinburgh. It has been immensely successful with Scottish audiences and this edition is complete with critical and historical notes and glossary.   £2.10*, 90p+

SCOTTISH PROSE 1550-1700
Edited by Ronald D.S. Jack

Contains writings by James VI, John Knox, Bishop Leslie, Lindsay of Pitscottie, George Buchanan, Drummond of Hawthornden, Sir Thomas Urquhart, Sir George Mackenzie and Samuel Rutherford.   £2.25*, £1.00+

SCOTTISH SHORT STORIES 1800-1900
Edited by Douglas Gifford

This collection gives a very wide picture of the Scottish tradition in fiction, and includes stories by Sir Walter Scott, James Hogg, John Galt, W.E. Aytoun, James Grant, George McDonald, William Alexander, William Black, Margaret Oliphant M.P., and Robert Louis Stevenson.   £2.50*, £1.25+

* Cloth   + Paper

Forthcoming Titles

SCOTTISH SHORT STORIES 1900-1970
Edited by Douglas Gifford and Kenneth Buthlay

A BRIDIE ANTHOLOGY
Edited by Ronald Mavor

SCOTTISH ROMANTIC POETRY
Edited by Alexander Scott

C AND B PLAYSCRIPTS

		Cloth	Paper
*PS 1	TOM PAINE Paul Foster	£1.05	45p
*PS 2	BALLS and other plays (The Recluse, Hurrah for the Bridge, The Hessian Corporal) Paul Foster	£1.25	50p
PS 3	THREE PLAYS (Lunchtime Concert, The Inhabitants, Coda) Olwen Wymark	£1.05	35p
*PS 4	CLEARWAY Vivienne C. Welburn	£1.05	35p
*PS 5	JOHNNY SO LONG and THE DRAG Vivienne C. Welburn	£1.25	45p
*PS 6	SAINT HONEY Paul Ritchie	£1.25	55p
PS 7	WHY BOURNEMOUTH? and other plays (An Apple A Day, The Missing Link) John Antrobus	£1.25	50p

		Cloth	Paper
*PS 8	THE CARD INDEX and other plays (Gone Out, The Interrupted Act) Tadeusz Rozewicz tr. Adam Czerniawski	£1.25	55p
PS 9	US Peter Brook and others	£2.10	£1.25
*PS 10	SILENCE and THE LIE Nathalie Sarraute tr. Maria Jolas	£1.25	45p
*PS 11	THE WITNESSES and other plays (The Old Woman Broods, The Funny Old Man) Tadeusz Rozewicz tr. Adam Czerniawski	£1.50	60p
*PS 12	THE CENCI Antonin Artaud tr. Simon Watson Taylor	90p	40p
*PS 13	PRINCESS IVONA Witold Gombrowicz tr. Krystyna Griffith-Jones and Catherine Robins	£1.05	45p
*PS 14	WIND IN THE BRANCHES OF THE SASSAFRAS Rene de Obaldia tr. Joseph Foster	£1.25	45p
*PS 15	INSIDE OUT and other plays (Still Fires, Rolley's Grave) Jan Quackenbush	£1.05	45p
*PS 16	THE SWALLOWS Roland Dubillard tr. Barbara Wright	£1.25	55p

		Cloth	Paper
*PS 17	THE DUST OF SUNS Raymond Roussel	£1.50	60p
PS 18	EARLY MORNING Edward Bond	£1.25	55p
PS 19	THE HYPOCRITE Robert McLellan	£1.25	50p
PS 20	THE BALACHITES and THE STRANGE CASE OF MARTIN RICHTER Stanley Eveling	£1.50	60p
PS 21	A SEASON IN THE CONGO Aimé Césaire tr. Ralph Manheim	£1.50	60p
PS 22	TRIXIE AND BABA John Antrobus	£1.05	40p
PS 23	SPRING AWAKENING Frank Wedekind tr. Tom Osborn	£1.25	45p
*PS 24	PRECIOUS MOMENTS FROM THE FAMILY ALBUM TO PROVIDE YOU WITH COMFORT IN THE LONG YEARS TO COME Naftali Yavin	£1.25	45p
*PS 25	DESIRE CAUGHT BY THE TAIL Pablo Picasso tr. Roland Penrose	90p	40p
PS 26	THE BREASTS OF TIRESIAS Guillaume Apollinaire	90p	40p
PS 27	ANNA LUSE and other plays (Jens, Purity) David Mowat	£1.50	75p

		Cloth	Paper
PS 38	DISCOURSE ON VIETNAM Peter Weiss tr. Geoffrey Skelton	£1.90	90p
*PS 39	! HEIMSKRINGLA ! or THE STONED ANGELS Paul Foster	£1.50	60p
*PS 41	THE HOUSE OF BONES Roland Dubillard tr. Barbara Wright	£1.75	85p
*PS 42	THE TREADWHEEL and COIL WITHOUT DREAMS Vivienne C. Welburn	£1.75	75p
PS 43	THE NUNS Eduardo Manet tr. Robert Baldick	£1.25	50p
PS 44	THE SLEEPERS DEN and OVER GARDENS OUT Peter Gill	£1.25	50p
PS 45	A MACBETH Charles Marowitz	£1.50	75p
PS 46	SLEUTH Anthony Shaffer	£1.25	60p
*PS 47	SAMSON and ALISON MARY FAGAN David Selbourne	£1.25	60p
*PS 48	OPERETTA Witold Gombrowicz tr. Louis Iribarne	£1.60	65p
*PS 49	THE NUTTERS and other plays (Social Service, A Cure for Souls) A.F. Cotterell	£1.65	75p

	Cloth	Paper
*PS 28 O and AN EMPTY ROOM Sandro Key-Aberg tr. Brian Rothwell and Ruth Link	£1.75	75p
*PS 29 WELCOME TO DALLAS, MR. KENNEDY Kaj Himmelstrup tr. Christine Hauch	£1.25	50p
PS 30 THE LUNATIC, THE SECRET SPORTSMAN AND THE WOMEN NEXT DOOR and VIBRATIONS Stanley Eveling	£1.50	60p
*PS 31 STRINDBERG Colin Wilson	£1.05	45p
*PS 32 THE FOUR LITTLE GIRLS Pablo Picasso tr. Roland Penrose	£1.25	50p
PS 33 MACRUNE'S GUEVARA John Spurling	£1.25	45p
*PS 34 THE MARRIAGE Witold Gombrowicz tr. Louis Iribarne	£1.75	75p
*PS 35 BLACK OPERA and THE GIRL WHO BARKS LIKE A DOG Gabriel Cousin tr. Irving F. Lycett	£1.50	75p
*PS 36 SAWNEY BEAN Robert Nye and Bill Watson	£1.25	50p
PS 37 COME AND BE KILLED and DEAR JANET ROSENBERG, DEAR MR. KOONING Stanley Eveling	£1.75	75p

	Cloth	Paper
PS 50 THE GYMNASIUM and other plays (The Technicians, Stay Where You Are, Jack the Giant-Killer, Neither Here Nor There) Olwen Wymark	£1.60	75p
PS 51 THE MAN IN THE GREEN MUFFLER and other plays (In Transit, The Sword) Stewart Conn	£1.50	60p
*PS 52 CALCIUM and other plays (Coins, Broken, The Good Shine, Victims) Jan Quackenbush	£1.80	95p
*PS 53 FOUR BLACK REVOLUTIONARY PLAYS (Experimental Death Unit 1, A Black Mass, Great Goodness of Life, Madheart) Leroi Jones	£1.25	55p
PS 54 LONG VOYAGE OUT OF WAR Ian Curteis	£2.25	£1.05
PS 55 INUIT and THE OTHERS David Mowat	£1.75	75p
PS 56 ALL CHANGE and other plays (Magic Afternoon, Party for Six) Wolfgang Bauer tr. Renata & Martin Esslin, Herb Greer	£2.00	95p
PS 57 CURTAINS Tom Mallin	£1.60	70p
PS 58 VAGINA REX AND THE GAS OVEN Jane Arden	£1.25	55p
*PS 59 SLAUGHTER NIGHT and other plays Roger Howard	£1.50	60p

		Cloth	Paper
PS 60	AS TIME GOES BY and BLACK PIECES (Party, Indian, Dialogue, My Enemy) Mustapha Matura	£2.00	£1.00
PS 61	MISTER and OH STARLINGS! Stanley Eveling	£1.75	75p
PS 62	OCCUPATIONS and THE BIG HOUSE Trevor Griffiths	£2.50	£1.00
PS 63	AC/DC Heathcote Williams	£2.25	95p
*PS 64	MR. JOYCE IS LEAVING PARIS Tom Gallacher	£1.95	80p
PS 65	IN THE HEART OF THE BRITISH MUSEUM John Spurling	£1.95	95p
PS 66	LAY BY Howard Brenton and others	£2.10	95p

OTHER C AND B PLAYS

		Cloth	Paper
Adamov, Arthur	PAOLO PAOLI		75p
	PING PONG and Professor Taranne	90p	60p
Antrobus, John	YOU'LL COME TO LOVE YOUR SPERM TEST (New Writers IV)	£1.25	85p
Arrabal, Fernando*	PLAYS VOLUME I (Orison, Fando and Lis, The Car Cemetery, The Two Executioners)	£1.25	85p
	PLAYS VOLUME II (Guernica, The Labyrinth, Picnic On the Battlefield, The Tricycle, The Condemned Man's Bicycle)	£1.50	75p

	Cloth	Paper
PLAYS VOLUME VII (Hunger and Thirst, The Picture, Anger, Salutations)	£1.50	75p
PLAYS VOLUME VIII (We All Fall Down, The Oversight)	£2.25	95p
PLAYS VOLUME IX (Macbett, The Vase, Learning to Walk)	£2.25	
THREE PLAYS (The Killers, The Chairs, Maid to Marry)		35p
THE BALD PRIMA DONNA (Typographic Edition)	£7.35	

		Cloth	Paper
Jupp, Kenneth	A CHELSEA TRILOGY (The Photographer, The Tycoon, The Explorer)	£1.50	75p
Mercer, David	THE GENERATIONS (Where the Difference Begins, A Climate of Fear, The Birth of a Private Man)		£1.20
	THREE TV COMEDIES (A Suitable Case for Treatment, For Tea on Sunday, And Did Those Feet)	£1.25	65p
	THE PARACHUTE with Let's Murder Vivaldi, In Two Minds	£1.50	75p
	RIDE A COCK HORSE	£1.05	

		Cloth	Paper
	PLAYS VOLUME III (The Grand Ceremonial, The Architect and Emperor of Assyria, The Solemn Communion)	£2.00	90p
Borchert, Wolfgang	THE MAN OUTSIDE		35p
Beckett, Samuel*	COME AND GO		45p
Duras, Marguerite	THREE PLAYS (The Square, Days in the Trees, The Viaducts of Seine-et-Oise)	£1.50	75p
	THE RIVER AND THE FORESTS (In the Afternoon of Monsieur Andesmas)		90p
Ionesco, Eugene*	PLAYS VOLUME I (The Chairs, The Bald Prima Donna, The Lesson, Jacques)	£1.75	95p
	PLAYS VOLUME II (Amédée, The New Tenant, Victims of Duty)	£1.75	75p
	PLAYS VOLUME III (The Killer, Improvisation, Maid to Marry)	£1.75	75p
	PLAYS VOLUME IV (Rhinoceros, The Leader, The Future in Eggs)	£1.75	75p
	PLAYS VOLUME V (Exit the King, The Motor Show Foursome)	£1.75	75p
	PLAYS VOLUME VI (A Stroll in the Air, Frenzy for Two)	£1.75	75p

		Cloth	Paper
Obaldia, Rene de*	PLAYS VOLUME I (Jenousia and Seven Impromptus for Leisure)	£1.65	75p
	PLAYS VOLUME II (The Satyr of La Villette, The Unknown General, Wide Open Spaces)	£1.75	
Pinget, Robert*	PLAYS VOLUME I (Clope, Dead Letter, The Old Tune)	£1.25	75p
	PLAYS VOLUME II (Architruc, About Mortin, The Hypothesis)	£1.65	75p
Walser, Martin	THE RABBIT RACE and THE DETOUR	£1.60	£1.00
Weiss, Peter	THE MARAT/SADE	£1.75	85p
	THE INVESTIGATION	£1.75	£1.05

* These authors represented for dramatic presentation by C and B (Theatre), 18 Brewer Street, London W1R 4AS